Enduring Wisdom

Life Insights That Stand the
Test of Time

Compiled by

Kyra Schaefer

Enduring Wisdom

Life Insights That Stand the Test of Time

Copyright © 2021. All rights reserved. The author is responsible for their individual opinions expressed through their words. The author retains the copyright to this book. No part of this publication may be reproduced, distributed, or transmitted to any form or by any means, including photocopying, recording, or other electronic mechanical methods, without the prior written permission of the publisher.

As You Wish Publishing, LLC
Connect@asyouwishpublishing.com

ISBN-13: 978-1-951131-26-5

Printed in the United States of America.

Nothing in this book or any affiliations with this book is a substitute for medical or psychological help. If you are needing help please seek it.

Table of Contents

Wisdom From the Spirit Realm
By Rollie Allaire 1

Two Different Kinds of Love
By Rose Bourassa... 15

It Is What It Is: Things I've Learned in Life
By K.C. Cooper 29

From Chaos to Emotional Freedom
By Beth Eiglarsh 43

Life, Love, Loss, Lessons
By Anne Foster Angelou.. 59

What's Your Story?
By Karen Gabler... 73

Love From Behind the Mask
By Foxye Brown Jackson... 87

It's Start Time: Fully Living through Life's Worst Fears
By Donna Kiel.. 99

Finding My Happy
By Amy I. King... 111

Generational Perspective
By Geneva Dantes... 123

Speaking Stones
By Becki Koon.. 135

Meaning Matters, Got Meaning?
By Paula Meyer... 149

The Wisdom Within
By Maggie Morris 159

Turtle Wisdom
By Vanessa Plimley 173

Don't Be a Knock Off, the Original is Always Better
By Samantha Renz 187

Is that Gucci Luggage You Are Carrying?
By Dr. Carra S. Sergeant 199

Say the Magic Words
By Lindy Chaffin Start 213

Seeking Happiness in Hardship
By Katie Tryba 227

A Rocky Road to Parenthood
By Dorothy Welty 241

Soul Signs
By Kristen West 255

Chapter

Wisdom From the
Spirit Realm
By Rollie Allaire

Rollie Allaire

Rollie Allaire is a Holistic Life & Wellness Coach whose Spirit Name is Geegado Megwan Kwe, which means Talking Feather Woman.

Since 2001, Rollie has drawn on her extensive career background of clinical psychotherapy skills and, in recent years, combined that with Energy Work, Chakra work, Crystal Reiki, ThetaHealing, Akashic Record reading and clearings, meditation, Moon Medicine teachings and looking at life through the Medicine Wheel in the form of Life & Wellness Coaching and Facilitating.

She helps women with anxiety by giving them the ability to soulfully master their emotions, connect to their true power and learn to feel better in order to take massive action in their life so that they gain confidence, feel self-assured, strong, happy and surround themselves with a supportive, connected community when they feel most isolated.

Rollie creates safe spaces both virtually and in-person for women to experience deep, life-changing transformations and healing. And she strongly believes that each person has the ability to heal themselves. Her job is to bridge the gap between the client and the methods that best suit their process. No matter what our experience in life, we can change our lives by taking action and not staying stuck. By helping ourselves, we help others who are struggling with similar experiences. No one comes through this world without struggle, but it's how we move through those struggles that get us to the other side.

She also owns Bridging the Gap Wellness Center in Haileybury, Ontario, where she works with other practitioners who provide their services within their small Northeastern Ontario community. She is a proud and loving mother of two adult boys, a wife, and a daughter. You can find Rollie at her website www.rollieallaire.ca or email at info@rollieallaire.ca.

Wisdom from the Spirit Realm
By Rollie Allaire

I rewrite this article in light of the Canadian news that 215 children were found in a mass grave at a Residential School in British Columbia. Some of the children found were no more than three years old.

The story of the Residential Schools is not my story. It is the story of my ancestors and my family. I am fortunate to not have had to live this experience or anyone in my immediate family. However, it has impacted my life.

Enduring is described as "existing or remaining in the same state for an indefinitely long time: abiding, continuing, durable, lasting, long-lasting, long-lived, long-standing, old, perdurable, perennial, permanent, persistent" (The American Heritage® Roget's Thesaurus). *Wisdom* is described as "the soundness of an action or decision with regard to the application of experience, knowledge, and good judgment" (Oxford Languages).

This is what my experiences have taught me. Enduring wisdom doesn't have to come at a great cost, but sometimes that's the circumstances. Over the years, I have learned more about my culture, and I put into practice the things that we were not able to be taught.

When I decided that I wanted to write in this book, I did not intend to take on any political stances. However, this issue is way too big not to address.

CHAPTER 1 | WISDOM FROM THE SPIRIT REALM

For those of you who do not know me or are new to me, my Spirit Name is Geegado Megwan Kwe, which means "Talking Feather Woman." My name was gifted to me by an Elder. The story is quite funny, but I will explain this a little further down the road.

When the murder of George Floyd happened in the United States, there were a lot of Canadians talking about how there was no discrimination in Canada. People were appalled by the mistreatment of the black people in such a diverse country as the United States. Canada is no different. The exception is ethnicity.

I wanted to take you on the journey of how I have been able to endure my wisdom in my short time on this earthly plane.

I remember when I was working at our local Women's Shelter back in 2001, and I first learned the "truth" about our "Canadian history" with First Nations people. We had an Elder come in and teach about the "Hidden Holocaust" right here in Canada. I was mortified to think about what was going on.

I knew about the last Residential Schools closing in 1996. Unfortunately, our government took very little responsibility, at least from my perspective. We hear how the churches are responsible for this genocide. However, it was the Government of Canada who wanted to "kill the Indian out of the child." This was quoted by Sir John A. MacDonald, who was our first Prime Minister of Canada. His plan was to remove the children from their parents to force them to assimilate as a "Canadian" in this "new" country. This country wasn't new; it was very much inhabited by what they referred to as savages.

As I shared, in British Columbia, the remains of 215 children were found. And some as young as three. People were mortified and shocked that this could happen historically. This isn't part of our history; it is part of our present.

In 1996 when the last Residential School closed, I was having my 2nd child. He is now a young adult. These children who survived the terror, torture, sexual, physical and mental abuse are part of this generation. These are parents or grandparents of the children my own children have grown up with. This isn't "past" information. Yes, it started in the 1800s, but it continued until the late 1900s. That's a lot of families being impacted.

These are human beings. And my ancestors. Because of these actions taken by the government, I continue to learn the teachings of our ancestors. We are fortunate to have some Elders who have been able to continue to pass on the teachings.

I was about 10 when my great-grandfather passed away. We grew up and lived in the City of Timmins, Ontario. As he became more and more ill, my great-grandfather would say, "On n'est pas des Indians," which means "We are not Indians." I never understood why he would say that all the time when we would go over. My thoughts were, "Of course not. We don't live on a reserve. We live in the city." "Indians" is a term used in the "Indian Act" to describe the First Nations people of Canada.

CHAPTER 1 | WISDOM FROM THE SPIRIT REALM

I also later learned about the '50s and '60s scoop, where children were taken from their parents and placed in "white" foster homes. My great-grandfather was afraid that would happen to his family and needed to be sure that we were safe. Until Bill C-31 in 1985, no one in our family had any "Indian Status" as his mother married a white man. Until this Bill, any woman who married a white man lost their status. However, if a white woman married a native man, she gained Indian Status. There were still more amendments made after that date to allow for inclusion.

Because we "grew up white," I was deprived of my culture. My grandfather practiced a lot of the medicines as he lived off the land. However, I didn't know when I was a kid that it was something to cherish because it wasn't known as being a traditional practice. If one of us were sick, he would go to the bush to gather things and make a batch of something to heal our cough or heal a wound. I wish I would have learned more about those medicines. He learned these things from his mother, who no longer had "status" at that time.

My grandfather was definitely a Healer. My grandfather and my uncle were working in the bush, and somehow, one of my uncles ended up with a severe cut on his leg. He was severely bleeding. My grandfather went to him and placed his hands on him, said a prayer, and the bleeding stopped. He told my other uncle to get him to the hospital. When they arrived at the hospital, the bleeding started again. I will never forget that story that my uncle shared as the doctor had shared that he had no idea how he didn't bleed out before he got to the hospital.

ENDURING WISDOM

Our family was fortunate because we are white-passing, so we didn't have to experience the discrimination that was and is still being experienced by my people. My great-grandfather's uncles' families were not that fortunate, some maintained their Indian Status, and now I know that he watched his cousins and his cousins' children be taken away. He wanted to ensure our safety.

My story is about having lost my culture, while many others were about losing their identity, living in fear, experiencing horrific traumas that they still carry with them and pass from generation to generation.

What really had me thinking was a video that I watched of a woman who immediately went to her mother after hearing the news. Her mother was a Residential School Survivor. She was talking with her about this finding of the 215 children. Her mother's response was astonishing. She said, "My Residential School was smart; they didn't bury the bodies; they burned them. They will never be found." And although I knew that as I heard that before, it was like the world stopped as I soaked it in, as if hearing it for the first time. Even though these stories of the brutality have been shared, there was no proof.

It continues to shock me, as I still cannot believe how inhumane people can be. When I hear people rave about how wonderful Canadians are versus Americans, I simply shake my head. There is such bigotry. If you do not fall under the "white persons" norm, then there is something wrong with you.

CHAPTER 1 | WISDOM FROM THE SPIRIT REALM

In spite of all of this, I have been able to gain some of this Sacred Wisdom, and I am able to pass it down to the next generations.

I shared earlier about my Spirit Name and said there was a funny story behind that name. The story begins with a Healer who started coming to a nearby community. I struggled with going to see this Healer for my own needs, as I didn't feel I was "aboriginal" enough to be worthy of his healing. I always attended his teachings, however.

In the group, I was always the one asking questions, sharing a statement (only when I had the Talking Feather), and I have (and still do have) a very inquisitive mind. One of the things that this Healer offered to do was to gift Spirit Names in Ceremony as many of us who would attend the teachings did not have our Spirit Name as it was not something that we were able to do, as Ceremony was forbidden in Canada for a long time.

I was so unsure of this as I am Metis, which means half-breed between another ethnicity and of aboriginal descent. It took me a long time to finally go to the Ceremony. My entire being was excited and fearful all at the same time. The Healer did the Ceremony as Spirit sent him my name. Geegado Megwan Kwe is my name. He shared what it translated to. I really wanted to show my appreciation and my excitement, but all that kept going through my mind was, "He thinks I talk too much."

As I was about to leave, he asked me to stay behind for a minute as Spirit had something for me. He ruffled around in his stuff, and he pulled out a feather. With all of the teachings that I received from him and from others, I knew that it was a great Honour to be gifted a feather. I was so thankful, but I didn't feel worthy. I really struggled with that. First, I get a name that I thought was derogatory because I was so inquisitive, but then I was gifted with this great Honour. I was so confused.

I took the feather and placed it inside my filing cabinet for many years. I was afraid to dishonour the feather. I practiced my name to get used to how to pronounce it and to be able to use it at some point, even though I didn't understand then what that meant.

Finally, one day, I "woke up" from my slumber. I received a message from Spirit that let me know what my name meant. It was about the knowledge that I have that I share with others. The feather also allows me to share its teachings with others.

Your feather and anything else you use in Ceremony or for healing is called "your bundle." Many of the teachings that I received were that you don't allow others to touch or use your bundles, that it's Sacred. I always had the urge to share my feather or my crystals or anything else that I use in my bundle. I had the opportunity to sit with a Grandmother and, of course, I was full of questions. One of the questions was about this urge to share with others. She shared with me that although we receive teachings from others, we also gain Wisdom from Spirit. The messages that I am receiving about sharing my bundle are because that is part of who I am.

My name doesn't mean that I talk too much, but that I need to talk, and I need to share what I know and what I learn. It is my responsibility to share with others. And she and other

CHAPTER 1 | WISDOM FROM THE SPIRIT REALM

Elders have taught me that I need to "take what I need" from the teachings and leave the rest. This is an approach that I use with my clients all the time. However, another Grandmother's teaching was that sometimes we need to be quiet to learn the lesson or to clearly hear what is being said. Sometimes even simply "absorbing it" so that you can process it is why silence is important.

As time passed and I continued to learn and share, I met up with a colleague who did a session where she connects with your ancestors who have passed on. She shared with me that there was an Aboriginal Man in full garb, including a headdress. I was intrigued. She indicated that he was telling her that he was my great-grandfather. Remembering the words of my great-grandfather in the last year of his life, I told her that it wasn't possible because he didn't identify as Native. I told her the story. She shared with me that he wanted to apologize for saying that to me. He wanted me to know that he was always with me. And he wanted me to know that he would be with me to teach me what I needed to know so that I can share my wisdom with others as this was my life's purpose.

He has come to me in other sessions with other practitioners at different times. I know that he is with me all the time. He also comes to my mom in her dreams when there is something going on with our family. I cherish his messages and his presence in my life. There is a strong connection with him as my mother is his first grandchild, and I am his first great-grandchild.

I love the fact that his message was that he will always be there to support me. In fact, our ancestors have been around for thousands of years and have a deep connection with nature. This connection allows us to heal. All things connect with Mother Earth. When we open our hearts to listen, the messages are clear.

It's important that we attempt to respect and restore Mother Earth. She is in such need of healing. In the year 2020, we've seen how slowing things down with planes, travel restrictions, and less commuting back and forth for work, Mother Earth has had the opportunity to heal. We need to think about the mechanisms toward the alignment of sustaining life. We need to look at how we as humans are perpetuating problems.

By embracing a more holistic life, we can see the kind of success that will bring healing into our world. The more in touch we can be with Mother Earth, the more in touch we can truly be with ourselves. When we actually hold the earth in our hearts and understand how to do the work to live in balance and in nature. It is not easy to live in balance. It requires some discomfort, sacrifice and the ability to recognize that there are parts of our lives that we need to unplug from and start again.

One of the things that is important for me is to bring women back into the center of society that will restore a healthy balance. It will allow us to truly "endure" the wisdom that we are meant to bring forward.

With this knowledge, I continue to learn more about my culture and teachings gaining more wisdom that I hold dear. I bring these forward in my life that allow me to be the best version of myself. Now, I am fully able to accept my own Wisdom as I am meant to. I carry my name

CHAPTER 1 | WISDOM FROM THE SPIRIT REALM

proudly and share my knowledge with those who cross my path.

One of the things that I have learned throughout this journey is the importance of believing in yourself and being who you are meant to be. It is not an easy path that we travel in this lifetime, but as Pierre Teilhard de Chardin shared, "We are not human beings having a spiritual experience; we are spiritual beings having a human experience." This means that before we were born into this physical plane, we existed in spiritual form. We are eternal Souls.

Meegwich (means thank you) for being part of my journey, and I wish you great peace in your life. Honour who you are. Be who you are.

Chapter *Two*

Two Different Kinds of Love
By Rose Bourassa

Rose Bourassa

Rose Bourassa is a retired procurement specialist and International bestselling author for her contribution to the books *The Grateful Soul* and *Ordinary Oneness*. She is currently preparing for a second career as an evidential medium and proprietor of a spiritual center. She is a wife, mother, grandmother, student, teacher, and volunteer. To keep sharp, she strives to learn something new every day. Hopefully, something to help keep up with grandkids. Even when they have to dumb it down! You can reach Rose via email at Remnick@aol.com.

Two Different Kinds of Love
By Rose Bourassa

The Legacy of an adopted child

Once there were two women who never knew each other,

One, you do not remember, the other you call mother.

Two different lives shaped to make yours,

One became your guiding star; the other became your sun.

The first gave you life, and the second taught you to live in it.

The first gave you a need for love, and the second was there to give it.

One gave you a nationality; the other gave you a name.

One gave you the seed of talent; the other gave you an aim.

One gave you emotions; the other calmed your fears.

One saw your first sweet smile; the other dried your tears.

One gave you up - that's all she could do.

The other prayed for a child, and God led her straight to you.

Now you ask through all your tears the age-old question through the years;

Heredity or environment - which are you a product of?

Neither, my darling - neither - just two different kinds of love.

Author unknown

CHAPTER 2 | TWO DIFFERENT KINDS OF LOVE

I am the one who prayed for a child, and God led me straight to her, the one that gave you up.

All my life, I wanted to be a mom. After seven years of trying it, we decided to adopt. My husband wasn't sure at first, but I went full steam ahead and contacted several agencies and acquainted myself with the procedures and fees. Then I told him we had an appointment with an agency, the very same agency my parents had been foster parents in my early childhood years.

The orientation meeting was brutal. Here sat this woman in front of 20 couples, all vying for a chance at parenthood. She spoke in a monotone voice, waving one arm to the left, the other to the right. We sat in our chairs, trying to stay awake. Could this get any more boring? Can you throw some hope our way? How about a smile? A change in vocal tone? Anything to tell me I made the right decision selecting this agency?

At the end of the meeting, we were handed a packet of document requests and forms to be completed. The process to be approved could take six months to a year. Oh no, you watch me get this done in record time! I've waited my whole life already. Do you think I will wait another six months to a year? Seriously? You must not know who you are dealing with, people.

With the packet completed, we waited on a call to set up our first in-person interview. It was like watching for the pot to boil. Not happening fast enough for me! When finally scheduled, we appeared on sight—bright-eyed, bushy-tailed and highly hopeful. Then the shoe dropped. Our counselor was none other than the monotone lady from the orientation meeting. This was a disaster in the making. After a two-hour conversation on our life and why we wanted a child, we discovered she was quite lovely. And not monotone at all. She'd just done that orientation lecture so many times before it was like being on auto-pilot.

We received yet another packet of forms to be completed. Letters of reference were needed, fingerprinting, background checks, physical check-ups. I couldn't comprehend why we had to go through all this stuff when the only thing the girls had to do was get pregnant! And by the way, "Were you married in the church?" As we were with a Catholic agency, where you married was a big deal. It seems a lot of those unwed mothers wanted their children to be placed in loving church-sanctioned homes. Add the seemingly impossible task of getting married in the church to the list.

One by one, we ticked off the items to be done. Getting married in the church was going to be problematic. My husband had been previously married in the church and divorced by the state. Now we needed to get his first marriage annulled. Not an easy task. We set the wheels in motion.

We continued with our interviews, together as a couple and then as individuals through all of this. Some of the questions revolved around discipline. "What are you going to do when your child spills the milk?" Well, I guess that depends on how old the child is and whether there is a

CHAPTER 2 | TWO DIFFERENT KINDS OF LOVE

worldwide milk shortage. I don't know. Make him/her help me clean it up? Use a sippy cup next time to avoid future spills? What kind of question is that? Lord knows it's not a capital offense. No corporal punishment will be involved, but I have a perfect corner already selected for time out! Wait, wait, wait, let me get my crystal ball out and polished up and see how I will handle the future situation. Is my answer right or wrong?

"Control yourself!" I said to myself. Giving these crazy answers wasn't going to get you a baby any faster. One wrong statement, and it could be game over. Lucky for me, the monotone lady wasn't taking me seriously and thought I was funny and laughed.

Along with the million hours of interviews, we had to attend classes with other hopeful parents. In our first class, we heard from a young woman who had given up her child for adoption and why she chose adoption as her plan. Then we heard from adult adoptees on what it was like growing up adopted. In another class, we dealt with different situations. Another round of "how will you handle this?" Hum, did I bring my crystal ball with me today? Then we were broken into groups to discuss potential outcomes.

In the situation groups, we were dads vs. moms. When brought back together in the group, we shared answers to see how different our parenting skills would be. I particularly liked the teen- year questions. That answer was easy—take away the car keys! Side note: not once in these classes did we cover how to reprimand the child who mooned his preschool class (yes, he did that) and do it with a straight face. "Mommy, am I trying your patience?" he said. It was Mommy who needed the time out after that.

Then there was the home inspection. "What? You need to see my house?" New panic attack.

We were remodeling the kitchen. The cabinet doors were up, unpainted and without handles. We hadn't babyproofed the house! We were going to fail for sure. It turned out okay. We had time to babyproof, and we had a room for the new baby—no bottom drawer in the highboy for our baby! And our handleless kitchen cupboard doors were considered babyproofed already since we needed a butter knife to open them.

It took us ten months to complete the process and get our formal approval letter. Then came the biggest challenge of all. Our profile: writing about us to entice some young girl that we were the perfect couple to adopt her baby.

We were allowed to brag about ourselves! No matter what I wrote, it didn't feel right. It took several attempts to come up with the perfect profile, but I did it. I wasn't comfortable bragging about us, so instead, I told our humble story as an outsider looking in. It made much more sense that way.

Once submitted, we started our wait. Like the squeaky wheel, I called to check in with our counselor once a week. I figured she'd eventually get bored with me calling all the time and give me a baby to make me go away! No such luck. During this wait time, we were able to get my husbands' first marriage annulled. We remarried in the church the day before our original anniversary date. We were nearing two years in the process at this point. (I have

CHAPTER 2 | TWO DIFFERENT KINDS OF LOVE

a new appreciation for the pregnancy of an elephant. Both of us expecting about the same amount of time.)

We received a call that a new class on shorter profiles was coming up, and one of us should attend. I went for class and stopped in to see my counselor, armed with a new church marriage certificate and the confidence I would never be able to condense our life story into a couple of paragraphs. She had a piece of paper on her desk. "By the way," she says as calm as a cucumber, "You were in a match, and you've been selected."

Pretty sure my scream was heard around the world. Or at least the entire building. We were finally going to be parents! Since I could read upside down, I read part of the paper and learned which hospital she would be giving birth in. I knew that hospital. I was born there. I knew the maternity ward well as I had been in nurses aid training there in high school. I learned first hand you never place a baby boy on the scale undressed. Duck and cover!

I was so excited to be an official expectant mother. When I got home, I called my BFF and said, "Hang up and call me back. When I answer the phone, I want you to say, "Hi, Mommy." It took her a minute to realize what I was saying, but she called me back and said, "Hi, Mommy." Those fantastic little words had us both in tears of joy.

The agency arranged for a meeting for everyone before the baby's birth. We showed up for the meeting. She didn't. It turned out she had gone into labor the night before. While we were waiting at the agency, she was at the hospital preparing to give birth, although we wouldn't know she had for 24 hours.

We had been too nervous for breakfast that morning. Unsure of what to expect. What if our birth mother didn't like us in person? So many fears to meet someone who held our dreams in her hands. We stopped at a restaurant on the way home. We were sitting in a window seat having coffee and pursuing the menu; there was an earthquake. I believe it was 9:08 a.m., give or take a minute. The restaurant manager immediately hurried us away from the window seat, along with several others. Once reseated and back to our coffee, another earthquake hit at 9:18 a.m. This day was off to a great start.

I had hung a pair of yellow baby booties on my office door as a sign to my co-workers we were about to have a baby. The next day after our scheduled meet and greet, I went to work. I alerted our telephone exchange operator (I know. I just dated myself big time.) that I was expecting a call from *that woman* who never gives her name and always says, "*It's a very personal call.*" Everyone knew who she was and why she was calling. There was no keeping this a secret in my office. This baby business was big news, and everyone was in on it.

The call finally came through just before 10 a.m. The operator transferred the call to my desk but didn't disconnect the line till she was sure I was at my desk to answer. It was a pleasant conversation. "Hi, how are you? I have some news." Yes? Spill your guts, lady! As she was telling me, "It's a boy," and providing all the vital statics, I looked over to the yellow booties. Everyone on my floor was standing at my office door, waiting as anxiously as I was for the news.

CHAPTER 2 | TWO DIFFERENT KINDS OF LOVE

"It's a boy!" I don't remember how long the jumping and screaming and congratulations lasted. It seemed like forever in no time at all. Remember the two earthquakes the day before? Our new son was born in between them. I think that was a sign he was going to shake up our lives! And so he did.

The agency scheduled a new meet and greet meeting. We had to meet face to face before we could take the baby home. Talk about being on edge! Somehow we all were seated together in the same room. One set of prospective parents, one young girl with her mother. Is that her? Our birthmother? Too nervous to start up a conversation. We would look at each other and look away when we got caught. We sat there for 30 minutes, not saying a word. Then her counselor arrived and was surprised we are already together. Why weren't we engaged in a conversation already? Two hours later, we parted with hugs and thanks. Two days later, we brought home our little bundle of joy.

For the next five years, we traded letters and pictures back and forth. For the adopted parent who wants to share every bit of her child's life but doesn't want to bore her friends to death, writing to her was an excellent way to communicate. Sending pictures of a happy little boy with big grins and cheeky cheeks helped his biological mother to know she has made the right decision to place her child with us.

Five years later, we decided to file papers for our second adoption. We had the family over for a BBQ. We shared we were planning on adding two feet to the family home. My little brother turns to me and says, "Why don't you just make one?" I looked over to my husband and asked, "Did your parents tell you how to make one?" "No. Did your parents tell you?" We both laughed and replied, "We don't know how!"

Our second adoption was so much easier. We joked that our daughter must have been conceived the same day we filed papers because we brought her home precisely nine months later. She was born with a congenital disability. We didn't care. We only saw a beautiful little child.

She'd been born with a bilateral cleft palate. Not the end of the world, but it made feeding a special event. Every two hours, she ate. To this day, she eats every two hours! There were doctor visits with a team of professionals and corrective surgeries on a very predetermined schedule. She had two sets of braces, not one, two. When she became school age, our daughter wasn't happy to miss school to go to the yearly cleft clinic. (I'll never get perfect attendance if you make me miss school!) We re-named the clinic the "check-up from the neck up" day and followed up the day with something special—lunch out, shopping. Whatever it was that made her happy. We went every year for 21 years.

It is incredible to see the advances in cleft palate repair over the years. You would never know there was ever anything wrong with that beautiful smile of hers. That smile would light up a room even before the first corrective surgery. Our counselor told us once that the love from a special needs child is like no other. We found this to be so very true. There is no measure to the joy and love she brings to our lives!

CHAPTER 2 | TWO DIFFERENT KINDS OF LOVE

We have always been open with both our children about being adopted since day one. Using the word adopted positively to let them know there is nothing wrong with being adopted. (Once, I told my son that adoption was God's way of saying it took two moms to create you. He formed you in one mother while you grew in my heart. Then God asked her to send you to me to love you for the rest of your life.) Both have been adult adoptee speakers for prospective parents groups. They both have had the opportunity to meet their biological mothers and siblings. Knowing how young these girls were when they made this monumental decision in life, it was nice to see how they have grown up and know the wonderful women and mothers they've become.

Somewhere in the master plan, I was meant not to bear children but to raise them. It makes no difference that they didn't grow in my womb because they grew in my heart.

We have so much respect for the two young women who decided to place their babies in the arms of these two loving parents. We are forever thankful for their decision to allow us to raise their child as our own. We hold them in a special place in our hearts. It takes a love of the highest power to want so much more for your child than you can offer and give your child up for adoption. There is no greater selfless gift anyone could have ever given us—the gift of parenthood.

Every adoption story is different. Some are easy, while others are hard. Some are long, others short. Some are open, others closed. Regardless of the path you took to adopt your child, one fact that remains constant—it will always take two different kinds of love.

Chapter Three

It Is What It Is: Things I've Learned in Life
By K.C. Cooper

K.C. Cooper

K.C. Cooper has been happily married for 26 years to a Veteran of the US Navy. She has four children and three grandchildren. She retired from the Arizona Department of Corrections after 30 years of service (7 years as a Correctional Officer and 23 years as a Legal/Resource Librarian). She is a small business owner, with a Small Business Management Certificate, and is pursuing a degree in Business Administration. She has a Bachelor's Degree in Biblical Studies, and is one of Amazon's Best-Selling

Authors in two collaborative books by As You Wish Publishing: *Love Meets Life* – Compiled by Tara Ijai, and *Ordinary Oneness* – Compiled by Kyra Schaefer. Upon completion of this article, she will be branching out as a solo author. She is a cancer survivor, and a spiritual person who seeks to fulfill her purpose in life by helping others through words, service, and life-changing opportunities. She became an activist for social justice in 2016, and has a desire to help women in abusive relationships. She is currently studying Black History to assist in improving the conditions of urban communities, and its people, and hopes to inspire others to make a positive difference in our society. In her spare time, she enjoys reading, writing, dancing, traveling, and spending time with family and friends. She can be reached at kcooper36@outlook.com.

It Is, What It Is:
Things I've Learned in Life
By K.C. Cooper

IDENTITY

If someone asks, "Who are you?" a lot of people tend to respond with their job description: a nurse, teacher, full-time mother, father, lawyer, doctor, and so on. When my college professor asked the class to answer this question in an essay, I think we were surprised when he chose to read one out loud. He didn't give the name, but he read it from beginning to end. It started with, "I am a strong and intelligent woman who is capable of accomplishing anything she puts her mind to." A part of me invisibly shrunk down in my seat because I had no idea an essay like that stood out amongst the rest. I remember the essay very well because it was mine. My faith was strong, and I had overcome many obstacles in my life. When the scriptures said, "I can do all things through Christ who strengthens me," and "No weapon formed against me shall prosper!" *I believed it*. I had set some goals for myself and was in the process of pursuing them.

What I didn't know was that my lack of knowledge in physics and biology would derail the course I had set for myself. By the time I got to macroeconomics on the business curriculum, I was overwhelmed and had to drop the class. I forgot I was utilizing the tuition reimbursement program through my employer, and the next few paychecks

CHAPTER 3 | IT IS WHAT IT IS

were a little lighter than normal. The instructor informed me afterward that he would have worked with me on the deadlines for submitting assignments, but when your plate is *full*, some things tend to fall off without notice.

Although I dropped out of college to relieve some stress, our church had a Bible college, and everyone was encouraged to attend. So, as one of the pastor's team members, I eventually enrolled. Many students (including myself) found the night school challenging due to raising children, household duties, financial obligations, and extra-curricular activities. However, I was determined to finish the three-year curriculum without stopping. My husband lovingly took on the full responsibilities in our home, and I pressed on with work and school. I stayed focused with the help of my family and completed the program. Unfortunately, my health continued to decline, and my identity began to shift.

"The only person you are destined to become is the person you decide to be." —Ralph Waldo Emerson

PURPOSE

Most of us tend to lead our lives day by day, with very little structure. Some of us have goals, but they are not written down with steps and time frames to achieve them. We carry out our daily duties hoping they will come true. We are so caught up in the status quo (the existing state of affairs) that we neglect to pursue our individual calling in life. Many of us have never taken the time to ask ourselves, "Why am I here?" But at times, the question lingers in our subconscious mind when we lay awake at night or find ourselves daydreaming.

I was one of those people in the rat race. I was spinning my wheels, doing everything I was expected to, except accomplishing my goals. When I finally got a chance to exhale, I learned that being busy does not equal progress. We can run on a treadmill and never leave the room. That's what my job felt like. Sure, I was earning enough to buy a house, cars, and other material possessions, but it was unfulfilling. My position and the atmosphere did not permit me to make a positive difference, nor was it a path I would have chosen for myself. However, the benefits and promotions kept me there.

When I began hearing and reading about purpose, it was as if a light bulb turned on in my head. I knew there had to be more to life than the mundane functions we performed on a daily basis. I became eager to find out what my purpose was in life. My daily prayers included asking God to help me find and fulfill my purpose. That's around the time when things began to shift, and not necessarily in a pleasant way. I stepped outside of my character and started speaking up about things I disagreed with. I stepped down from certain duties in the pursuit of seeking balance. I started making my health and happiness a priority, in spite of the expectations of me, and then the unthinkable happened. My greatest fear came upon me. A few of my closest relatives passed away within a short period of time, and I was trying to cope under pressure. By the time the second funeral came, which was my father's, the bow broke. I was *no longer in control* of what I said or did. The restraints were

CHAPTER 3 | IT IS WHAT IT IS

off, and I was *forced* to be liberated from the opinions of people. The details will be shared in my memoir.

As the pieces of my life began to unfold, I could see the trail from a distance that led me to this place. I know it was my prayers that took me out of the rat race and placed me on the *path* to destiny.

> *"Too many of us bury our dreams in a lesser existence, making ourselves a graveyard of God's precious treasure."*
> —Dr, Myles Munroe

HEALTH & WELFARE

Even Wonder Woman and Superman get tired and have to rest sometimes too. We can't be everything to everyone and still have gas left in the tank for ourselves. We have to know when to step back and refuel. Whether it's with an afternoon nap, a slow walk on a nice day, a good read, a massage, a hot bath, a girls' or boys' night out, or a weekend getaway. Whatever we consider to be our cup of tea to unwind and relax from the demands of life, that's what we need to do on a regular basis. Some of us may need that escape once a week, a month, every other month, or every 3-6 months; it all depends on our individual health, lifestyles, and budget.

Unfortunately, I learned this way too late. I was working a full-time job, trying to be a good mother, wife, daughter, sister, and friend, and somehow, within a short period of time, I had six different assignments in the church while trying to go back to college to pursue a degree in business (which was one of my goals). I became a living example of the old saying, "pressure will bust a pipe!" The injury I sustained as a teenager unknowingly had residual side effects. The complications eventually led to early retirement from my career in law enforcement, numerous exams, medications, and surgery. If we don't pay attention to the signs our body gives us when we need a break, we run the risk of it malfunctioning on us.

Imagine that we are like a vehicle. We can only go so far before we need to refuel. But remember, although gas can be interpreted as energy, we still need to monitor the oil, transmission fluid, water in the radiator, battery life, headlights, brakes, and so on.

Our health determines the quality of our life, and based on our age, genetics, environment, and personal choices, time may not always be on our side. So, we need to eat right, get plenty of sleep, and go to the doctor for regular check-ups (especially if something doesn't seem right). Just as a car will give you a notification that something is not operating properly, our bodies will too.

So, before you (or someone you know) begins to short circuit, step back and re-evaluate your priorities. Is there anything on your list that can be eliminated? Can you reduce the amount of time you spend on certain tasks? Are there duties you can delegate to someone else? And if you can't do something, simply say, *"I can't,"* and let your "No" mean *"No!"* If someone asks, "Why not?" Or says, "That's not fair!" Simply say, *"It is what it is!"* A timely no to someone else is simply a yes to ourselves. Yes, to peace of mind.

CHAPTER 3 | IT IS WHAT IT IS

I spent years trying to regain my focus after adjusting to my new limitations. It took a while before I recognized the magic word that I needed to understand earlier in life. It was *balance*. If we put everything in perspective, we can lead a healthy and balanced life.

Over time, I have embarked upon a spiritual journey that has been both liberating and fulfilling. I have done my best to eliminate judgment. Although I still have some work to do in that area, I no longer believe that everyone should think and believe the same things as some of us are taught. I don't believe our creator had an assembly line in the reproduction or birthing process. Everyone is equipped with their own gifts, talents, and abilities to fulfill their purpose in life and is entitled to their own opinions and beliefs. As long as their actions do not bring harm or ill will towards others, we should all be able to live peacefully with one another.

> *"The real winners in life are the people who look at every situation with an expectation that they can make it work, or make it better." —Barbara Pletcher*

My new motto is *"Live & Let Live!"* I don't care if you're black, white, blue, green, brown, or yellow; Christian, Muslim, Buddhist, Atheist; Republican, Democrat, or Liberal. As long as you treat people right, you're okay with me.

FINANCES

There is an old misinterpretation that says, "Money is the root of all evil." Well, most people have learned the true meaning of that quote. It is not money itself; it is the "love" of money that causes people to do evil things to get it (or keep it). We have to be willing to work hard to get the things we want, and knowing how to manage our money is a key part.

Although I've been a saver most of my life, the American educational system has *not* taught us financial literacy. We have had to learn to balance a budget, calculate interest rates, investment procedures, the mortgage lending process, and so on, on our own. Many of us are usually between 30–60 years of age before we understand that our credit score is a reflection of our financial integrity and can hinder us greatly. If we owe a debt, we should pay it when it's due. Failure to do so can create limitations in acquiring the things we want in life. Our credit report is simply a list of creditors telling other creditors whether or not they can trust us with a loan.

My problem wasn't not having a good credit score; it was not knowing how to use it to my advantage. I also learned that co-signing is not a wise decision. Therefore, based on my lack of knowledge, I could have been a business owner much sooner and had more in my investment accounts. Which in turn would have increased my potential of becoming a philanthropist.

> *"It's easy to make a buck. It's a lot tougher to make a difference."* —Tom Brokaw

CHAPTER 3 | IT IS WHAT IT IS

EDUCATION

Education is defined as the process of facilitating learning or the acquisition of knowledge, skills, values, morals, beliefs, and habits. Unfortunately, this process has allowed others to teach us *what* to think instead of *how* to think. We memorize answers to questions and are promoted based on our ability to recall the information. Therefore, our nation is built with more followers than leaders.

"By working faithfully eight hours a day, you may eventually get to be boss and work twelve hours a day!" — *Robert Frost*

However, there are a lot of people who did not finish high school or college and are in the top one percent of the US population of wealth (because they think outside of the box). They utilize their free will to follow their own intuition, unique ideas, and God-given talents to specialize in a particular area of expertise.

> *"Education distinguishes between those who know and those who do not know. I have learned that education is beyond what you learn in school and books; it is also what you learn from life. Informal education has taught me that no matter how much I may distinguish myself, it does not make me better than anyone else."* —Chad J. Kyles

Although education does not make anyone better, it does have the potential to make one wiser. It can be described as having a deep understanding, a keen sense of discernment, and the capacity to exercise sound judgment. Education also has the ability to improve one's quality of life through better health, social circles, positive experiences, and advancement opportunities. I love learning and plan to be a student for life, and what we don't know can hurt us.

SERVICE

I have learned that what we do for others is oftentimes more important than what we do for ourselves. However, we do need to make sure that we are taking care of ourselves in the process. I heard someone use the analogy of giving in the form of a water hose (I won't quote them because I don't know who the originator was), but the statement said, "In the process of delivering water to someone or something, the hose gets wet too." Another example is, "You have to be blessed with something first before you can bless someone else with it." These examples are part of the universal laws established in the earth.

- Sowing & Reaping – Give, and it shall be given unto you.
- Gravity – What goes up must come down.
- Karma – Every action must have a reaction.
- Compassion – Do unto others, as you would have (it) done unto you.

All of my life, my greatest fear has been public speaking, but later, I learned that a lot of people were interested in what I had to say. As an average individual, I didn't think my opinion mattered, but I discovered that it is our unique experiences in life that give us a different perspective. In turn, those different viewpoints can be used to help us shape our current realities. For example, the fight against poverty, domestic violence, alcohol and drug abuse, and many other issues are often fought by people that have been affected by or overcome them.

CHAPTER 3 | IT IS WHAT IT IS

When I started college, I began pursuing a degree in counseling. I wanted to help people cope with the challenges they faced in life. Although I had seen and experienced a lot growing up, I was pretty even-keeled on my outlook in life. I maintained a demeanor of calmness and self-control. I don't recall ever letting my emotions get the best of me. But after completing my pre-requisites, I took a class called Chemical Dependency 101. What I didn't know was that a lot of the students in the class were recovering addicts. I eventually learned that I may have been able to help someone manage their emotions, but I was unable to help a recovering addict fight the cravings that could lead to relapse. Many of the students felt they could not receive from someone who had not been in their shoes before. I didn't even have an addiction to candy, sodas, cake, ice cream, or anything. The closest thing I had to addiction was sweet potato pies during the holidays, and I knew how to fight that craving after a few slices too many. So, I ended my pursuit of a counseling degree and changed it to business. Looking back, I think being a counselor could have added a lot of stress to my life because I discovered I am an empath. I have a tendency to feel the pain of others (almost literally). However, business was a field that I could keep a poker face in and continue my desire to learn.

Nonetheless, wherever we happen to find ourselves in life and the challenges we face, it does us no good to cry over spilled milk. Clean it up and keep going.

Our goals don't care how we feel, so we might as well suck it up and press on! Whether it's losing weight, getting a particular job, obtaining a degree, or running a marathon, stay focused and keep going. Just accept the fact that *it is, what it is!*

"In three words, I can sum up everything I've learned about life: It goes on." —Robert Frost

Chapter Four

From Chaos to
Emotional Freedom
By Beth Eiglarsh

Beth Eiglarsh

Beth Eiglarsh, a self-proclaimed perpetual student, was born with a gift of compassion and sensitivity, which served her as she ascended the corporate ladder. After years of success in the travel and advertising industry, she decided to pursue a dream by founding her own company in 2003. The Julia Taylor Collection, lovingly named after her daughter, specializes in custom, one-of-a-kind works of art, designed and hand-crystallized. Her work was featured all over the US and Caribbean and was included in the

Oscar and Grammy celebrity gift baskets. A global partnership with Bacardi placed her VIP gifts in Dubai, Abu Dhabi, France, Norway, Poland, Australia, Thailand, and the UK.

In 2009, Beth was drowning in workaholism and found herself operating from a place of chaos, fueled by fear. After hitting her *rock bottom*, followed by intense introspective work, Beth was gifted the opportunity to realign with her essence, purpose, and mission. Today she is a Certified NLP Life Coach; a Certified Spiritual Healer; an Advanced Practitioner Reiki Master in Usui, Kundalini, and Lightarian healing modalities; a Holographic Memory Resolution trauma therapist, and a Healy Quantum Healing energizer. Her motivation is simply to help people feel better. Her greatest passion comes from empowering others to see the world and themselves in a more positive light via the mind, body, and spirit. She's a master perspective shifter who facilitates awareness, healing, and permission to be your true authentic self. Beth draws on her gifts as an empath and intuitive to help her clients unfold and expand into the very best version of themselves. She adores her husband, three children, and precious Goldendoodle, Angel.

Beth currently offers one-on-one sessions, workshops, A.R.M.S. training courses, and Mind, Body, Spirit retreats. Join Beth's community at www.SpeakToBeth.com

Contact:

305 613-3298

Beth@SpeakToBeth.com

www.Facebook.com/SpeakToBeth

From Chaos to Emotional Freedom
By Beth Eiglarsh

"Enduring wisdom is sitting still while your pain quietly transforms into purpose." ~ Beth

"I want a normal mommy, and if she's not normal, I want her to go back." That was a recorded message from my seven-year-old son Evan when I was whisked away to a treatment facility in October 2009. Unable to think or use my phone, I couldn't recall how and why I was being transported from a detox center in Miami to a rehab facility in West Palm Beach.

The recording continued. "Mommy's always stressed, and when she gets stressed, I get stressed," exclaimed my five-year-old Julia.

I had no idea how my actions had been affecting my children. My three-year-old son Owen was as clueless as I hoped he would be when I dropped off the face of the earth and left their lives for an eternity.

I worked to overcome my stage fright when I had to pee in a cup in a small bathroom while being chaperoned. While I trudged through embarrassments that nightmares are made of, my suitcase was being dumped and scrutinized. My phone, money, and reading material were confiscated. After that shocking admission process, I began having severe

CHAPTER 4 | FROM CHAOS TO EMOTIONAL FREEDOM

heart palpitations. I insisted my blood pressure be checked to ensure I wasn't having a heart attack.

While others were assigned individual rooms, I was held "under watch" in the main house until my emotions stabilized. That took four days.

Where am I?

How did I get here?

Why am I an hour away from my husband and 3 children?

Over the following two months, my family became a distant memory. I closed my eyes and tried to remember the sounds of their voices.

After two weeks, I was permitted to make one ten-minute phone call on Saturday and another on Sunday. The sound of the timer's buzzer burned like an arrow in my heart. I was forced to hang up on those I loved.

That was it! That was my bottom—the beginning of the fog lifting—so I could finally look in the mirror and see into my soul.

> *"When you realize how perfect life is, you'll tilt your head back and laugh at the sky."* ~ Buddha

I am beyond grateful for the clarity that crystallized through my experience. Buried in the intense emotional and physical pain was the key to my happiness. A radical shift in thinking emerged from that transformational voyage that enabled me to see how truly perfect life is. It *all* made sense! We are here to expand through a tangible experience—to explore a life that is deliberate, a journey that is fulfilling, and a legacy that is evolutionary. We are here to learn and to love, and enjoy. To awaken to that realization, we must go through a metamorphosis. Only then can we reveal our innate calling and a more astute direction. Moments of discomfort and struggle offer beautiful opportunities to understand ourselves better. Times of confusion and crossroads are the vehicles that carry us to greater destinations. Hardships that kick us out of alignment with our core being are designed to shake things up so that we can settle where we belong. When I look back on my impending doom, I see that a greater design was always working in my favor.

To step into my role as a life coach and teach tools for transformation, I needed to transform myself. To provide an illuminated path for others to see their way back to the light, I had to navigate the darkness. To facilitate energy healing, I needed to understand my energy and the role it plays in my overall well-being. To teach my clients how to re-evaluate their foundation, mine needed to crumble. *Because* of my story, I'm a more valuable contributor to the world. My conviction that this is the case for everyone motivates me to want to help others view their life stories from a new angle. One that shifts the dialogue from "Why me?" to "Whom might I be able to help?"

If you are currently enduring (pain) wisdom, congratulations! While it may not feel warm and fuzzy at the moment, you are well on your way towards the next phase of your development. Whoo-hoo! The universe is always privy to the blueprint of your soul and is continuously working *with* you and *for* the highest good. Maybe you began to veer away from your soul's quest? Possibly the

CHAPTER 4 | FROM CHAOS TO EMOTIONAL FREEDOM

heaviness of life prevented you from reaching your dreams? Perhaps your discomfort is less about the issue you are facing and more about what you are avoiding? I have found that the most profound growth spurts lie in what I fear the most. Once I developed a courageous heart, I was able to walk through the rubble and build a new, unbreakable foundation.

> *"Wisdom is the bridge between chaos and emotional freedom." ~ Beth*

After living through my most challenging moments and making it to the other side, scathed (transitive verb: to damage something by blasting or scorching it. see also: to subject somebody to severe criticism), I realized that my story, itself, was a curriculum in the making.

My spiritual awakening was a call to action to help others awaken to their best selves. I developed a four-step process that offers transformative tools to facilitate the journey of self-discovery. It holds your hand and walks you through the key components for living your most authentic human experience. Implementing these steps into your daily life helps you achieve a new perspective, a dose of positivity, and a pathway to your purpose.

My A.R.M.S. System for Living offers you the keys to unlock your hidden gifts and the freedom to unwrap the present. A.R.M.S. is an acronym that stands for AWARENESS, REMEMBER, MANIFEST, and SERVICE. Why the name? The fact that your arms belong to you is a fundamental message that *you* are the sole person responsible for your happiness. If you follow your arms to the center of your being, they lead to your heart, where all things are possible.

Our arms are an extension of our body which houses our entire being: thoughts, feelings, organs, molecules, blood vessels, etc. How we think can affect our bodies, and our bodies can affect how we think. Oftentimes, after some revelation, groundwork, and personal growth, we are still met with unsettled emotions and unwelcomed symptoms of dis-ease.

I've done the work; why do I still feel like crap?

Our bodies are the articulation of unfinished business and unhealed trauma. Understanding the mind-body connection is critical in healing all aspects of our whole self. The A.R.M.S. system engages the mind, body, and soul for a tested and proven strategy that will catalyze your transformation. Covered in its entirety in my book, *Beth's Case Scenario*, here is a glimpse of the process and how you can use it to embrace yourself lovingly and fully.

A - AWARENESS is everything. You can't move toward a new reality if you don't know where you are. Begin by identifying the major categories of your life and establish your satisfaction in each area. Where are you spending too much time? What areas of your life might require a little more nurturing? Become aware of what's important to you and then cross-reference your schedule and make sure you are incorporating those elements or activities into your life.

Become aware of your energy, your thoughts, and your emotions to determine what feels good and what needs to change. Pay attention to how you speak to yourself and how you react to others. Awareness will inspire you to offer compassion and understanding in every situation. Practice giving people the benefit of the doubt, understanding that everyone is fighting a battle that you may be unaware of. Become a fly on the wall of your life and witness yourself in action.

Understand that all the players in your life are there to reflect back to you your strengths as well as your weaknesses. Thank those who ruffle your feathers because they have brought forth that which needs attention.

Take responsibility for your happiness. Don't wait for someone to bring you joy on a silver platter. Go and get it! Find opportunities to dance or belly laugh or sing. Your life is happening *right now.*

All spiritual journeys begin with awareness. What feels like a mess turns out to be a message. Become aware of the big picture by broadening your vision. Align with the solution by making sure your environment, thoughts, and actions support where you want to be. Don't be afraid to make adjustments and ask for help. That is courage. That is growth. That is awareness.

Awareness Exercise: Go one full day without complaining about anything. (No aches, pains, weather, co-workers, politics, etc.) Not even negative self-talk, because shh, you're listening! Without judgment, use this powerful and revealing exercise to become aware. Jot down your experience.

_____

_____

_____

R = REMEMBER who you were before the world molded you into who you are today. You are a spiritual being having a human experience who came here to learn, reflect and expand. Look in the mirror and remember your essence, your light, and your true nature. You are a unique individual expression of the universe. The world needs your distinctive offerings.

Remember to peel off the labels that you've adhered to that don't belong to you. Break free from people, places, thoughts, and things that no longer serve you. Eliminate the masks, obligations, and people-pleasing, and treat yourself to the word "no." Let go of the need to be understood and just be you.

Stop looking to become something. Look to return to yourself. Remember that you chose to incarnate, to add your colorful string to the collective tapestry. In moments of exhaustion, remember that you're surrounded by an unlimited supply of strength, from the seen and unseen world, fueling the back of your heart with unconditional love.

You may be challenged to overcome situations, but remember that was part of the plan. We are presented with what we need for our soul's growth. Those obstacles are springboards. Remember that you are powerful beyond measure! Allow your pain to create a bridge, leading you to a greater destination.

CHAPTER 4 | FROM CHAOS TO EMOTIONAL FREEDOM

Remember, there is only one you. You are deeply loved, and you are here on purpose. Remember who you are. Then own it, live it, love it, and be it!

<u>Remember Exercise</u>: Imagine yourself with layers upon layers of clothing, representing obstacles, limiting beliefs, others' energy, and anything weighing you down. Set your alarm for five minutes and close your eyes. With each exhale, let go of a virtual layer of clothing. With every inhale, supercharge what you love and admire about yourself. What did you uncover?

_____
_____
_____
_____
_____

M = MANIFEST your dreams by becoming an energetic match to what it is that you want. You are a super magnetic creator of your reality! Based on the law of attraction, the universe will always support where you are vibrating. Are you thinking about what you want? Or are you focusing on what you don't want? Use my G.O.A.L.S. method as a quick and easy reference to attract anything and everything you want.

> *G = GET CLEAR.* Visualize specifically the outcome you desire. See what you would see, hear what you would hear, and feel what you would feel. Become energetically aligned with your vision.
>
> *O = OBSTACLES.* Eliminate them. Fear keeps you on the edge of the diving board, scared to jump. Squash any doubts that you deserve your desired

outcome. Believe that you are here to accomplish and move mountains. That's why they are in front of you.

A = ACTION! Words mean nothing unless followed by intentional movement. Action is the deliberate creation of your future! Every. Single. Day. Take a step toward that goal, even if it seems insignificant. No matter what, keep moving.

L = LET GO. Develop a healthy dance between momentum and non-attachment. Plant your seeds, water them, and nurture them, but don't keep digging up the roots to check the progress. Over-care can be unhealthy. Have faith that something better might be growing.

S = SUPPORT. Develop an honest support system that offers strength, encouragement, and accountability. Lean on your spiritual support team who are pushing you towards your greatest accomplishments. Surround yourself with those who believe in you and keep you on track.

Manifest Exercise: Identify what you want. Jot it down below with great detail. Decide what action step you can take *today* toward that goal. Do it! Then give yourself a well-deserved hug.

What do I want?

_____

_____

CHAPTER 4 | FROM CHAOS TO EMOTIONAL FREEDOM

_____

_____

What baby step can I take today to support that?

_____

_____

Action completed. (date) _____

$S = SERVICE$ is a two-part process designed to echo our ultimate mission on earth. Service to self anchors us in an ever-changing world. Nurturing your mind, body, and spirit by recognizing and honoring your needs perfectly positions you to be of service to another.

Service to others is about connection and compassion. It allows you to offer value to another person's existence by extending your energy through thoughts, time, or money. It whispers, *"I see you, and you matter."* Service blurs the lines, allowing us to dissolve our differences and identify our similarities. We are all in this together.

Ask yourself, *"What do I need to find my peace?"* Then ask, *"How can I help someone find theirs?"* That is service.

<u>Service Exercise</u>: A random act of kindness expands your heart, releases feel-good hormones, and instantly aligns you with source energy. Surprise a stranger today with a compliment, a coffee, a love note, or a meal. Describe your experience below.

_____

_____

_____

_____

_____

Master Perspective Shift

Do not get discouraged! Healing is a lifelong process of constant re-evaluation, re-calibrating, and re-applying the solution. Use the A.R.M.S. method to navigate life's unexpected twists and turns with ease. Shift from frustration to acceptance, imbalance to balance, and from chaos to emotional freedom while learning to love your whole self in the process. If you knew in advance that you signed up to be your own Indiana Jones, exploring new terrain, escaping killer boulders, and finding love, you could allow yourself to have more fun on your journey, despite the bruises, snake pits, and broken hearts.

While your individual story is unique, your emotions are not. They reflect your internal narrative and, once harnessed, can be the roadmap to a life of sustained joy and inner peace. Recovery from any setback is a slow process involving self–reflection, self-forgiveness and self-love. I did the work as if my life depended on it. As a result, I rediscovered *me* and learned to love myself, as is. You can, too!

Problems are the solution. How can life be a carnival without rollercoasters? How revolutionary would the *Wizard of Oz* have been if Dorothy had clicked her heels three times at the end of the first act? We are not here only for smiles, achievements, and rewards; we are here to

CHAPTER 4 | FROM CHAOS TO EMOTIONAL FREEDOM

embrace and fully appreciate those smiles, achievements, and rewards. It takes being hungry to appreciate being satiated. It takes sadness to appreciate feeling happy. It takes experiencing failure to value success. It takes enduring wisdom to reveal our greatest strengths.

Begin today. This moment. Because after all, *this moment* is the only one that exists. And it's the only place that happiness can be accessed. Don't be afraid to come undone. Get excited to be the artist of your revised masterpiece. Eliminate the elements that you have outgrown. Add your favorite resources and brighten the colors! Become your favorite work of art.

My system for living is the wisdom I earned, from the lessons I endured. The sum of its parts is the meaning of life.

To be *aware* is to be alive.

To *remember* is to give life meaning.

To *manifest* is to contribute to life.

To *serve* is to love life.

Thank you for allowing me to wrap my A.R.M.S. around you.

In gratitude,

Beth

Chapter Five

Life, Love, Loss, Lessons
By Anne Foster Angelou

Anne Foster Angelou

Anne lives in Seattle, WA, with her Greek spouse of 48 years and reached her 77th birthday last November 2020. She has lived a long life with many challenges, losses, accomplishments, joy and a blessed opportunity to sing as a professional opera singer for 20 years at Seattle Opera. She worked full-time as a public servant for over 40 years in the daytime and sang at night. She has a B.A. in The Art of Performance, a Certificate in Records and Information Management, a Certificate in Private Investigation and was trained as a Master Home Environmentalist Volunteer for the American Lung Association of WA. She loves learning new things every day, laughter and enjoys and celebrates the joy and accomplishments of others. Take charge of your life. Celebrate your gifts. Get the help and love you need to overcome hurt. Anne has more stories to share and hopes you do too. She loves other cultures, languages and cats. This is her 4th collaborative book with As You Wish Publishing. Email:

fosterangelou@comcast.net.

Life, Love, Loss, Lessons
By Anne Foster Angelou

Since COVID, who has not been preoccupied with death and the urgency to live fully in the moment, to mend what is broken, to change what can be changed and to accept what is unalterable? It is a daily awareness and focus. Get the house in order, love more fully, clear away the obstacles, both physical and psychological. Remove the focus from "things" and credentials to love, forgiveness and taking care of each other.

My wisdom is not yours, but there is a commonality to learning, knowing, and coping in new ways when the same challenges arise. There is nothing unique in my knowing. My wisdom formed who I am today, and the work is not finished. My beliefs and opinions have been formed, honed and incorporated into my behavior. That does not mean I cannot change. New information, a better way of coping, more comfort in my life—all can effect changes.

I was going to name this article "Sex, Religion and Politics" which would surely get attention but also be relevant. They are triggers for argument, but it's a good starting point. Sex is how we got here from the passion of two people joining and enjoying their bodies. Sadly, for some, it was obligatory, but for others, ecstasy and orgasm were surely the motivation. As children aging toward puberty, we explored our own bodies in secret, driven by hormones (nearly always the culprit). Depending on parental nurturing, we either learned shame and guilt or

CHAPTER 5 | LIFE, LOVE, LOSS, LESSONS

were encouraged in healthy exploration. One of my maternal aunts revealed many years ago that when she caught her daughter playing with herself, she beat her. Is this where religion enters?

I was born into a poor Catholic family and prepared for my First Communion by having my First Confession (now called Reconciliation) around the age of eight. I was one of those diligent children who took seriously the "Examination of Conscience." I carefully went through the checklist and thoroughly took responsibility in great detail for how I had sinned. Then I would sweat and quiver while waiting in line before entering the dark cubicle with the sliding door. My heart would pound when I saw the door was open and the priest announced his presence. Then I would describe most delicately my sexual encounters with myself. Later in my mid-20s, in discussing Confession with neighbors, the women would laugh and say, "You told *that*? We never told that!" I was a good girl, and even after making out at a drive-in movie and steaming up the windows, I would never go further and just knew the lightning bolt would come out of the sky and strike me dead. My maternal grandmother and guardian never said that, nor did any priest or nun, but, in my mind, it was a probability. The frightening judgment and admonishment came when I was 18 and had met my future husband and, after two weeks, I dared to tell the truth: "Bless me, Father, it has been two weeks since my last confession and, since then, I have had sexual intercourse 18 times."

All hell broke loose! "Who is this young man! You must break off your relationship. You have ruined all chances of a spiritual, marital union with him!" I said, "But we're planning to be married." "Oh no, you're not." In my naïveté, marriage was what you do once you've done the deed. I don't remember what penance I received or if I performed it. I remember telling Jeff what the priest said. He was not religious at the age of 19 nor in his life after that. I'll spare you the details of our sex life but suffice it to say we liked each other. The wisdom I gained from that relationship was that no matter how wonderful your body feels, it's "real love" that matters. There can only be so much sex. Kindness, respect, trust, honesty, vulnerability, and cherishing your beloved and wanting them to be well, happy and safe are so much more valuable.

Politics? Just vote and do the right thing for the good of all. No elaboration here.

I left home at age 19 in 1963 with all the possessions I could carry in a trunk and suitcase. My new home was thousands of miles across the country in Seattle, WA. From early childhood, my life experience had frequent trauma from violence, alcoholism and mental illness—the environment from my grandmother's children. She had her own issues, but alcohol was not one of them. She had a tragic life and died nine months later in 1964. To this day, I think I caused it—guilt from leaving her alone. If I had not escaped, I am sure I would not be alive today.

I went alone to my next life experiences that were painful, frightening and brought depression and anxiety. I was in a strange City and State with only my spouse, in-laws, co-workers, new neighbors and friends. As I have said, "I got by with a little help from my friends." Ill-advised or not, I adored Jeff, and the world revolved around him. He was

CHAPTER 5 | LIFE, LOVE, LOSS, LESSONS

psychologically controlling, possessive, secretive and, as I found out, very self-absorbed. It didn't help that he was brilliant, introverted, a talented writer and poet, handsome and very charming. We met at USF in Tampa, FL. He decided to return to the Northwest, and I insisted on following. He did not object, but I was not invited. I sought employment but, with no work history, I was not successful. He complained that if I did not work, he would have to drop out of school. Yes, I was a working wife supporting a student spouse. I returned to USF in Tampa, FL, for another trimester and bravely returned to Seattle seeking employment again. This all occurred before my grandmother died in August of 1964.

Wisdom: It was not obvious to me how self-centered my husband was nor how needy and dependent I was. His words, "I love you," ceased. He dropped out of school and had his tuition refunded that I had paid. He planned hitchhiking trips around the country and to Central and South America without me. He left and returned when he wished. He got involved in drugs in the 60s that caused Hepatitis C that lay dormant and eventually killed him when he was 73. I cried a lot, and when he said he wanted a divorce, I was stunned and terrified. I did not learn of some of his childhood trauma until after his death in December 2015, when I reconnected with his sister. When alone together or with friends, I had one personality with him and another when he was not around. I was my true self—playful, funny, creative, affectionate. I was so intimidated by his intelligence that there was no room for my own. One woman friend from Belgium said, "You're so much fun. Why aren't you like this around Jeff?" I said, "He doesn't like it." He remained affectionate and was never physically abusive but still distanced himself emotionally. The separation was inevitable. He packed and walked down the stairs, looked up at me to say goodbye, left, and when he arrived in California, he contacted me and said, "I don't know what to think, I haven't heard from you." Duh! In a phone call, he invited me to join him in Mexico for two weeks between Christmas and New Year's Eve in 1968. We had a lovely time, and then, on the way to the airport on New Year's Eve, he said, "Don't forget, I still want a divorce." I returned to Seattle, and he continued on to Peru accompanied by another woman, a part of his secret life. When he returned from Peru and wrote from California, I hastily flew to the address on the envelope in Venice Beach only to find no one home. A neighbor told me that he and Patricia were out to dinner. I met her the next day with an even more broken heart, but I guess some lessons are extremely difficult. When you have no family to guide you, it's even harder. Luckily, his parents were very helpful and supportive. I have described this contribution to my enduring wisdom because it was a very significant part of and one-third of my life. I believe that lessons learned hurt like hell but endure.

I learned later in some physical relationships that it's not the same as loving someone, not at all. Vocal performance and acting helped distract me from depression. Creativity took my concentration away from the pain. After my divorce, I returned to my University of Washington studies in Theatre and Music while working full-time until the final quarter before graduation. In September 1972, I auditioned for Seattle Opera and was hired for the professional

CHAPTER 5 | LIFE, LOVE, LOSS, LESSONS

resident chorus for the next 20 years. I met Dimitris in August of the same year, a month before. I graduated in 1973 with a B.A. in The Art of Performance and wrote my thesis based on an actor's journal and my first professional Actor's Equity Contract tour.

With my new love, my challenges were the Greek culture as well as a new language. I was also so intent on being independent after my divorce and so sure I never wanted to be controlled again that I was probably a challenge. We both were. We married in 1974 and made it through the last 48 years, sharing, caring, laughing and still loving each other. All our immediate family members have died. Dimitri's parents, siblings, aunts and uncles, a nephew, and dear Greek friends are gone. I have two aunts left, one in England (my father's sister) and one in Miami (my American mother's sister). My brother and I shared a mother but different fathers. We hardly know each other, unfortunately. I gained a Greek family, have visited Greece many times and have a functional knowledge of Greek.

Wisdom: Don't die with your music inside. Live your dreams.

Wisdom: "The key to happiness is giving up the need to (1) control others; (2) judge others; and (3) to be right." We will break the rules, be reminded and start all over again.

Wisdom: Human beings are the most dangerous animals on the planet. Make a difference. Come from a place of love. Do not support any harm, pain, discrimination, homophobia, racism, or any kind of separation or elitist entitlement.

Wisdom: We are here to love and take care of each other. See the divine in others and a reflection of yourself.

Wisdom: You will be hurt and hurt others. Do your best to be kind.

Wisdom: Love is not conditional; it isn't for some and not for others. Love is love, and all are worthy.

Wisdom: All humans want and deserve to be loved, safe, well, sheltered, clothed, fed, educated, and to have medical care in order to survive and thrive.

Wisdom: Life is not complete without playfulness and laughter.

Wisdom: There will be losses—humans, animals, devastation of the earth (natural disasters). Loss of employment, income, economic status, talent. Count your blessings and be a blessing for others.

CHAPTER 5 | LIFE, LOVE, LOSS, LESSONS

Wisdom: Give up blame and shame. We are largely responsible for things that happen to us except what we truly had no part in. We make choices, and they have consequences.

Wisdom: Forgive and pray to be forgiven. We are not blameless, but we make mistakes.

Wisdom: The way others treat us rarely has anything to do with us. That doesn't mean it hurts any less. They are their issues. Think before you act.

Wisdom: Meditation and prayer are good for the soul. Sincere and heartfelt connection to the divine is the goal.

Wisdom: Take care of your temple, your physical body. Feed it non-toxic and nutritious food. Move your body. Give it fresh air, clean and filtered water. Don't engage in addictions. Get help with your struggles.

Wisdom: Don't harm humans, animals or the earth. If you can live in this way, I don't care what you believe (faith, religion).

Wisdom: Love yourself. This is the hardest one since many of us were raised to believe this is selfishness (a negative connotation).

Wisdom: Tell your story; you deserve to speak it and for it to be heard. We all learn from each other's life experiences.

Wisdom: Breathe deeply when you feel sad, angry, or afraid.

Mourning the Loss of a Significant Friendship

The distant past, an old wound revisited when by chance, I learned of the death of my estranged friend's younger brother several months ago. I met "J" when he was 15 as a member of the Seattle Opera Chorus. Six months later, he got his driver's license, and we carpooled to rehearsals and performances. Our friendship was atypical since I was 20 years older but shared vocal talent, performance employment, a sense of humor and vulnerabilities (private pain and trauma). I helped him through struggles with his parents, who never accepted his sexuality, even after his chosen life partner died from AIDS. I think the best he could do was say, "My roommate died from cancer."

He was there for me through many life stresses: a major employment lawsuit, the murder of my mother, losing my opera contract after 20 years and an unsuccessful audition. I was his friend through bare feet, shredded clothing, tattoos, piercings, pink and purple hair and was a guest artist at one of his recitals. He moved to NYC, and we continued our long-distance friendship. Before he left, I hired him to give him some office experience that enabled him to be employed elsewhere in Seattle. They gave him a transfer

CHAPTER 5 | LIFE, LOVE, LOSS, LESSONS

opportunity, and he said, "…my salary will be much higher than yours." We laughed. We showered each other with gifts on birthdays, holidays (even Halloween). There is no room in the house without visible gifts as well as a stack of letters with encouragement and love. I had horrible menopausal symptoms with mood swings, hot flashes and night sweats that seriously impacted my behavior and health. I also discovered after years of depression and anxiety in the darker days of winter that I probably had SAD (Seasonal Affective Disorder). I don't encourage excuses, but this was my reality.

It was birthday time, and no package or card had arrived in the mail. He called me on my birthday and said he was taking a friend to the opera that night to thank him for a lovely day in the botanical gardens. It was a new gay friend, and he expressed apprehension at connecting and said he wasn't ready to date. I encouraged him, saying he needed friends and didn't need to make it a live-in commitment. Days later, I had an intense argument at home that triggered childhood trauma. I immediately wanted comfort from my dear friend. I was hysterical and spewed abusive nonsense into his answering machine. He wrote a letter a week later saying goodbye with no loving words, cold and final. That was in November 1996. His mother, who still lived in Bellevue, told me, "He says you write to him, but he never opens your letters." I wrote emails and letters. Letters were returned, as were packages.

His brother died in April of 2020. I wrote sympathy cards to his brother's widow, his mother (both in Cincinnati, Ohio) and to him. No one answered. I guess the deadliest blow of shunning me the rest of my life is his choice and my punishment. It hurts. He said years before, "If you ever cross my father, he will cut you out of his life and never look back." His father was his role model. Dimitri was so kind to me, trying to explain J's trauma and limitations.

Wisdom: You cannot be responsible for another's behavior or choices. You can be sorry and apologize but cannot expect forgiveness. Some people just can't do that.

Wisdom: Take what you have learned and mend your life. Do better next time. Make better choices so you don't hurt so much. I need to take my own advice.

Chapter Six

What's Your Story?
By Karen Gabler

Karen Gabler

Karen Gabler is an intuitive mentor, psychic medium, teacher and inspirational speaker. She also is a contributing author in seven internationally best-selling books on personal growth and spiritual practices. Karen is passionate about encouraging others to release the anchors that hold them in place, discover their soul purpose and live their best lives. While mentoring her clients through a variety of personal and business challenges, Karen combines her practical experience, developed over almost 30 years of legal practice and business coaching, with her natural intuitive ability to receive and utilize information and guidance from higher sources. She also facilitates soul readings to provide guidance to clients regarding their life path, and mediumistic readings to connect her clients with their loved ones in spirit. Karen conducts workshops, presentations and spiritual services on a variety of personal development, spiritual and business topics. She earned her Bachelor of Science in psychology from the University of Hawaii and her Juris Doctorate from the William S. Richardson School of Law at the University of Hawaii. Karen has pursued nearly a decade of wide-ranging education in interpersonal development and the spiritual sciences, working with numerous tutors from the prestigious Arthur Findlay College for the Psychic Sciences in England as well as intuitives, psychic mediums and spiritual coaches throughout the United States. She has been a WCIT in the Martha Beck Wayfinder life coaching program, and taught transcendental meditation as a student teacher at the University of Hawaii. She enjoys reading, hiking, horseback riding and spending time with her husband and two children. You can find more information about Karen at www.karengabler.com.

What's Your Story?
By Karen Gabler

"There are times in our lives when we have to realize our past is precisely what it is, and we cannot change it. But we can change the story we tell ourselves about it, and by doing that, we can change the future." —Eleanor Brown

Storytelling is central to our human existence. It enhances social cooperation and teaches us how to operate safely within a society. Stories allow us to build human connections by increasing our understanding of others. They allow us to understand our place in the world, and to find order in our experiences.

We also tell ourselves stories about our own lives and experiences. We tell ourselves stories about the traumas we have suffered, the way we've been treated by others, the losses we have experienced and what we believe we can or cannot do. We are limited in our ability to control the events of our lives, but we have the power to define our stories about those events. The manner in which we wield that power has significant impact upon our lives.

A decade ago, I lived under the shadow of my traumatic history. If you asked me about my life, I would tell you that I grew up without my father, having lost him before I was two years old. I would also share that my grandmother and mother both developed terminal cancer; they died within the same year when I was only 23. A year later, my boyfriend of three years developed leukemia. I married another man at age 30, but divorced three years later. My second husband required two heart procedures in less than five years. My son is diabetic, and my daughter was rushed to the hospital in an ambulance after a major seizure.

Because this was "my story," I walked through my life under a cloud, wondering when the next shoe would drop. When my husband was 20 minutes late from work one day, I suffered a near-panic attack, positive that he must have been in an accident and would never come home again. When he was in a rare bad mood, I worried that he was angry with me and could leave me at any minute. When my children wanted to spread their wings and try something new, I cautioned them about the dangers that could befall them out in the world, dampening their enthusiasm for new ventures. My sincere love for my family was tempered by an unhealthy dose of fear; I was afraid to let others into my heart because I worried that they would ultimately leave me heartbroken in one way or another.

One day, as I was chatting with a friend, she listened to my sad tale with widening eyes. She said, "That sounds like a tough beginning. It must be such a relief for you to feel safe and happy in your life now." I stared at her blankly, feeling as if she had thrown a bucket of cold water on me. I didn't feel safe or happy at all! How could I, knowing that something bad could happen to me at any moment?

Our conversation reverberated in my head into the following weeks. I began looking closely at the story I had been telling about my life. The moral of my story was, "I can't be happy. I'm not safe. Bad things always happen to me." The energy of this story followed me from one crisis to the next as I braced myself to "get through" the next challenge. As a result, difficulties seemed to crop up continuously. Mulling over the language I used as I discussed my past with my friend, I suddenly realized that my last major loss had been more than 20 years ago, and my last traumatic experience had been more than five years earlier. I enjoyed many moments of joy in between those difficult moments in time. And yet, I continued to describe my life as though it was nothing more than a series of tragedies.

With a great deal of inner exploration and self-development, I began to challenge myself to tell a different story. I looked closely at the blessings of my life, and the miracles that blossomed from the most devastating experiences. I re-worked the language I was using, focusing on my ability to overcome difficulty and the strength I had developed along the way. I wrote and re-wrote my story, developing empowering language to describe my gratitude at the path my life had taken.

Today, I would tell you that I was blessed to have been born to parents who loved me dearly. Yes, my father passed when I was young, and I cherish the photos of him holding me with shining eyes and a bright smile. My mother and grandmother had cancer at the same time, which gave them the unique opportunity to share their experiences and lean on each other during challenging treatment protocols. I was fortunate to have them with me for as long as I did, and I carry the lessons they taught me and the love they gave me inside my heart. I had a boyfriend in school who developed leukemia; he was lucky to fully recover after a successful bone marrow transplant. My first husband asked me to move with him from Hawaii to the mainland; I know now

CHAPTER 6 | WHAT'S YOUR STORY?

that our short-lived relationship was meant to take me across the ocean to California, where I later met and married the love of my life. My dear husband has been fortunate to catch unexpected heart issues early; he was able to obtain excellent medical care and is now healthy and happy. Our son has grown into a caring and responsible young man who serves as an example for others by seamlessly incorporating his diabetic procedures into his life. My daughter completely outgrew her childhood seizures; she is a remarkable young woman who is now an award-winning student, designer and author. The moral of my new story is "I deserve happiness. I am safe, and my loved ones are safe. I am surrounded by love, and always will be."

When narrating a new story, we must remember that the stories we have been telling ourselves aren't entirely false; they are always rooted in the truth of the events that occurred. My life is my life; the events I described above actually occurred and no amount of revision will change that. When you want to edit your story, it is important to honor your emotions and fully process the trauma you have experienced. Shoving the story into the recesses of your mind does not revise or improve the story. Instead, it merely lodges the story in your subconscious mind, endlessly informing and impacting your future.

That said, however, your emotional response to a present situation typically is generated by the story you developed after a prior negative experience. For example, imagine that you were laid off from your last job position. Naturally, this event caused stress and fear. To process those feelings, you created a story that you're not good enough to hold a job and you will always be at risk of being fired. At your next place of employment, you turn in your first project. The following day, you pass your new supervisor in the hallway and she does not acknowledge you. Your heart begins to pound as you wonder whether she is upset with you. "She must have hated the project. She thinks I don't know what I'm doing. I bet she's going to fire me!" When your past narrative is "I failed," or "they won't like me," you are unable to consider possible explanations for your supervisor's behavior that do not involve your failure. She may have been distracted, going through problems at home, or not feeling well. She may not even know that you have turned in a project. Your work may be exceptional, and she could be relieved to have you on her team.

This does not mean that we must pretend that key events in our lives never occurred—but it also does not mean that we must tell our story through the lens of pain, sorrow and loss. There are the facts of what occurred, and then there is our perception of those facts, which in turn creates the stories we hold within. The manner in which we tell our story impacts our experience of that event; we can relive the pain repeatedly as we repeat the same tale. More importantly, the stories we tell ourselves impact the energy we carry with us into the future. They can support our growth, or hold us in place. Creating a new story requires that we refocus our energy on the learning, the growth, the self-exploration and the gifts that come from the events of our past.

The first step in developing a revised narrative is to become aware of the stories you carry within you. What stories have you told yourself? Have you decided that you aren't

CHAPTER 6 | WHAT'S YOUR STORY?

creative or intelligent? Are you unlovable? Are you unable to control yourself around food or money? Are you unreliable or selfish? Pretend that you are writing a chapter in your autobiography, and journal about an event that was traumatic or difficult for you, or a situation in which you felt you failed yourself or someone else. Write a story describing those events, without censoring your words or trying to sugar-coat your experience. Write it as you feel it, using the first thoughts that come to mind.

Next, you must be willing to experience your narrative with fresh eyes. What is the story you are telling yourself? Is it empowering or disempowering? Are you the victim or the victor? Journaling about the situation and the feelings you've experienced allows you to discern where your thoughts are rooted in a story that no longer serves you. Carefully review each sentence you have used to tell your story, and ask yourself detailed questions: "Is that true? Not true? Where did I first learn that?" Identify where your narrative diverges from reality, or where you have drawn a conclusion about yourself based upon incomplete information or words once said by another. Look for sweeping statements or overgeneralizations, such as "I always..." or "I'll never...." Question the premises upon which you have based your story, and recognize that you hold the power to adjust your own narrative.

You can enhance your self-reflection by using additional writing prompts to excavate past events that subconsciously feed your self-talk. Ask questions such as: "When someone is angry with me, I feel _____," "When someone ignores me, I feel _____," "When I break a promise I've made to myself, I feel _____," "When I hear that someone else has succeeded, I feel _____." As you answer each question, take a moment to become aware of the memories that come up for you. Think back to your childhood to find the experiences that helped create your story. There may be more than one story that surfaces; choose the one that comes up first or feels most impactful. Journal about that memory. What happened, and how did you feel? How do those feelings compare to your present narrative?

Working with a coach or therapist also can assist you in clarifying the root of your negative story. When your stories are ingrained in your internal mind chatter, it can be difficult to recognize the core beliefs that have sustained your false narrative. A neutral observer can more easily recognize when you begin to express sentiments rooted in negative self-talk, and then guide you through an exploration and release of the genesis of those beliefs.

Once you have a good understanding of the stories you are telling and the experiences that allowed you to develop those stories, the next step is to actively create a new story. To develop a narrative that supports your highest good, you must start from the assumption that you are worthy of happiness, love, joy and abundance. Turn a discerning eye upon your ingrained beliefs: is it really true that you are unlovable? Is it really true that you don't deserve happiness? What story would you tell if you were lovable and happy? Delve into the positive qualities you have taken from a negative experience. Did you become more resourceful? More empathetic? More tenacious? More caring?

The words you choose for your new story are critical to developing a narrative that moves you forward instead of

CHAPTER 6 | WHAT'S YOUR STORY?

holding you back. Choose action words that describe what you want, instead of focusing on what you don't want. Is your story one of deprivation, lack and failure? Can you turn it into a story of redemption, vibrance and power? If you believe you'll never find love, your old story might include statements like, "I'll never meet the right person," or "It never works out for me." Your new story could include statements like, "I've learned so much about myself from my past experiences," and "I'm excited to meet someone new." If you believe that financial abundance is always out of reach for you, your old story could include statements like, "I can't save money," or "I never have enough." Your new story might include: "I have always been able to take care of my needs," and "I am excited to explore new ways to generate income." If you have tried 100 different diets without success, your old story might include statements like, "I'm a failure, I can't control myself around food," or "I just have no willpower." Your new story might be, "I know what my body needs," and "I can choose to eat healthy foods to nourish my body and increase my energy."

Personal mantras or affirmations can be powerful in this process: "I am worthy of being loved unconditionally. I am deserving of joy and happiness. I have everything I need." Just as the negative stories we tell ourselves can have a devastating impact on our mental and emotional health, using positive mantras on a daily basis can have tremendous power in altering our mindset.

Physical tools also may help you to envision and enforce a more empowering version of your story, particularly when your story is embedded in emotional attachment. Methods proven to break down resistance to a revised belief system include meditation, yoga, breathing exercises, and Emotional Freedom Technique, also known as tapping or psychological acupressure.

Once you have developed your new story, take concrete steps every day to bring that story into reality. Start and end your day with your personal mantras, engage in physical action steps that solidify your efforts, and journal about your experiences and thought processes. When reacting to a particular situation, notice the things you are telling yourself. Catch your negative self-talk and turn it around by asking, "What if?" What if your supervisor is upset about a personal issue and isn't thinking about you at all? What if the next person you meet is one who will shower you with love or become a fantastic new friend? What if you choose a healthy meal and your body feels alive and vibrant? What if a crisis occurs and you handle it with ease because you are incredibly strong and resourceful?

Most of all, don't beat yourself up because the false stories you've told yourself have impacted the way you have moved through your life. Remember that you have absorbed information during life events and developed narratives merely to protect yourself—emotionally, mentally and physically. This is an act of strength, not weakness, and you deserve to be celebrated. Be compassionate with yourself as you acknowledge that the stories that protected you in the past no longer serve you or your life path. Release those stories gently, thanking them for serving your needs at the time. Take control of your life by deciding what you want to bring forward with you as you reach for your dreams. When you let go of stories

CHAPTER 6 | WHAT'S YOUR STORY?

which are no longer needed and create an empowering narrative for your future—a narrative rooted in truth and supportive of your highest and best purpose—you can achieve everything you desire.

Chapter Seven

Love From Behind the Mask
By Foxye Brown Jackson

Foxye Brown Jackson

Foxye Brown Jackson is a two-time international bestselling author, Registered Nurse of 23 years, Sexual Assault Nurse Examiner of 3 years, Master Reiki practitioner, certified youth coach and mentor, and community advocate. Additionally, she holds a Bachelor's in Psychology, is pursuing her Bachelor's in Nursing, and is the founder of I Speak Foxye, a nonprofit organization for sexual assault awareness, prevention, and healing. She spent many years helping people transition from life through death; now, she helps them transition from death through life. Her everyday goal is to create a safe space for others to facilitate the transformation of their traumas into wellness.

Aside from her passion and purpose, she fills her spare time with magic! She enjoys reading so much that she created the Book Review for the Soul, which features a discussion, meal, and teaching surrounding incorporating the contents of the book into everyday life. Her spiritual self loves doing intuitive card readings, teaching spiritual and metaphysical topics, and embracing the energy of nature. She loves time at the beach, time with family, and watching movies. She lives each moment through the deeply held belief that everything and everyone is part of one energy, connected, and necessary.

Contact her by visiting her website at www.ispeakfoxye.com or emailing her at contact@ispeakfoxye.com.

You may also follow her on Facebook, Instagram, and Twitter as @ispeakfoxye. Get the latest video updates by subscribing to her YouTube channel, I Speak Foxye.

Love From Behind the Mask
By Foxye Brown Jackson

We are part of everything and everyone because we are all connected. That is what I will start off with. This is sometimes the hardest truth because we all want to believe that we are only part of those things that resonate with the *good* parts of who we perceive ourselves to be. However, we are connected to the homophobic, judgmental, racist, condemning religious fanatic, bank robber, murderer, sexual predator, manipulative, and exploitative ones as well. We are also connected to the peaceful, loving, inspiring, accepting, empowering, intuitive, and healing ones. We are connected to the victims of alcoholism, substance abuse, fear, low self-esteem, poor self-image, self-doubt, and unhealed trauma. The plants, animals, poor, rich, homeless, sheltered, satiated and hungry are all connected. Once we realize the truth of these connections, we will begin to expand our ability to heal the global consciousness.

The global consciousness is the interconnectedness of everyone and everything in the world. It is the spiritual thread that holds together the fabric of our universe. Understanding that this thread tethers all things together helps us realize how loving ourselves mends the tattered places in this quilt of life. This tattering has been created by traumas, including grief, disappointments, abandonment, loneliness, misunderstandings, and misplaced pride. It is

CHAPTER 7 | LOVE FROM BEHIND THE MASK

acceptable and great to extend love to those experiences and allow love to replace these feelings and emotions.

It has been often said that the greatest action is to love. I receive an immediate response when I ask, "What is your name?" However, that response is delayed when the question is, "What is love?" They often sit in silence for a moment to search for an answer. "An action," "An emotion," "A commitment" are the answers thrown into the dead space. There is a hint of uncertainty. A hint of embarrassment for not knowing what the true and complete answer is.

Over the years, my description of love has been altered by the wisdom of experience. I have progressed from viewing love as a feeling, an emotion, and an action based on the language I was speaking at the time. Meaning, if I was honing in on the love language of action, then my definition reflected actions that proved to me someone loved me; if it was the language of feelings, my definition reflected how someone made me feel. Through many moments, hours, and years of searching within myself to excavate the greatest version of self, I have concluded that love is a state of vulnerability. Love is opening oneself up to being emotionally vulnerable.

A first notion, when considering the state of being vulnerable, is to imagine the many instances of heartbreak caused by grieving over seemingly misplaced love. Remember, we are all connected, so everyone and everything is worthy of love. However, we would do well to understand that the definition of loving someone frequently becomes infused with false expectations. One such falsehood is that to love someone means you have to stay in close contact with them.

Many individuals are remaining in unhealthy relationships because of their perceptions of love. They sometimes feel that leaving the relationship equates to not loving the other party. That is untrue. Loving the other person means being vulnerable enough to let that person go. It means giving that person the needed space to progress toward self-love. Those who are abrasive and abusive to others are lacking the ability to truly love themselves. They cover this void with sadness, anger, narcissism, and explosive emotional acts. Certainly, loving oneself is the precursor to loving someone else.

Give love to self first, and it will trickle down to others. Give love to others first, and you will forever be indebted to self. If you have a basket of tulips and I ask you to give me a sunflower from your basket, you cannot give me one because your basket is filled with tulips. Likewise, if your spiritual vessel is not full of love, you cannot give that which you have not. Even if you have a portion of love in that vessel, once you give some to another, you remain indebted to yourself because you started with a deficit. What does it look and feel like to love yourself without a deficit?

The same energy used to extend love to another person is the same energy, multiplied, that you would use to love yourself. For many, extending love to another person involves sacrificing wants, providing basic necessities of life, embracing, kissing, encouraging, forgiving, supporting, speaking words of affirmation, answering the

CHAPTER 7 | LOVE FROM BEHIND THE MASK

phone when it rings, teaching, laughing, crying, spending money, quality time, and passing on words of wisdom. In essence, loving ourselves looks the same way: giving all these things to ourselves.

Many say they love their parents, grandparents, children, or spouses more than themselves. This is unfair to those in line to receive such love. It is unfair because if love is prioritized to these persons before self, the love is incomplete, deficient, and lacking in wholeness. Imagine the energy available to embrace someone after sufficient rest compared to that available after an extended day of manual labor. The latter may be weaker and followed by a sigh, indicating the body needs to *blow off* exhaustion. Whereas the former may be accompanied by a longer embrace, a genuine smile, laughter, a second embrace, conversation, a walk, and a completed task for the person receiving the love. This is possible because the vessel is at a capacity of overflow, and the love can flow from within to the outside. Loving from a self-love deficiency is likened to sailing in a ship that has a hole in the hull. Eventually, the waters of life will overtake the ship if the leak is not repaired. Repairing the hole is always detrimental to the life of the ship, just as repairing the lack of self-love is detrimental to your life.

As a nurse and a healer, I often see the outcomes of living a life of loving others before oneself. This does not translate to not loving other people; it is simply *first* loving yourself, just as you would want first to put on your life jacket *before* getting into the water. Deficiencies in self-love often create diseases and illnesses in the body (vessel), further making it difficult to give to those you desire to love. Therein lies the additional importance of prioritizing self-love. You deserve to be filled with love the same way you pour love into others.

James Baldwin stated, "Love takes off the masks that we fear we cannot live without and know we cannot live within." With this statement, a life partner sent me these additional words, "Love is an agent of change. It is something to be used to move toward freedom." Fear of what others think and long-held beliefs are two concepts that created multiple masks for me. I once avoided speaking about the details of my sexual assault because of fear of being the recipient of victim-blaming and victim-shaming. Simultaneously, I was in turmoil behind the mask of a *cookie-cutter* sexual assault story. Once I began pouring love into myself, practicing forgiving myself, and pampering myself with positive energy, I was able to build up my love stores and move toward the freedom of living without the mask. Indeed, I was able to love from behind the mask.

My first step of loving from behind the mask was to make a sign that said, "Operation Freedom." Then I began to journal my feelings and emotions, when I was happy or depressed, and when I had notable experiences which I wanted to remember. For every belief held, I searched for its roots, sought to understand why I believed that way, contemplated if it was a belief that resonated with my authentic self, and then decided on what *I* believed as opposed to what I was *taught* to believe. Removing that mask opened up a levee that allowed more love to flow within me than ever previously. That additional filling of

CHAPTER 7 | LOVE FROM BEHIND THE MASK

love was and is necessary to completely remove the remaining masks.

I have not been able to completely remove the fear-of-what-others-think-of-me masks. Instead, I gradually chisel pieces of it off. I have two major masks remaining, and it is becoming more exhausting to "live within" them. My solution was to seek the help of another healer: my therapist. Over the years, I have used my money to donate to organizations, buy clothes for charity, give as gifts, invest in my nonprofit organization, and many other noble and great things. When I realized the masks of my mental health and my sexual health were causing me to store the valuable essence of love in a place of decay, financially investing in my wellness became the highest priority.

Every healer needs a healer. Prior to being matched with my therapist, I had been learning to trust my intuition, building a relationship with my spirit guides, and understanding the spiritual purpose of my existence. I created a list of important characteristics I desired in a therapist. A primary characteristic was that they would not make me feel judged negatively for being who I am. I asked for guidance from my spirit guides and scrolled over the photographs of those offering counseling services. I tuned in to my intuition and asked for confirmation of which one I was matched with. When I got to the one who received a positive nod from the spirit guides, I disagreed and kept scrolling.

In hindsight, the notion that I disagreed with those from whom I had asked for help is quite hilarious. I searched that same site on several different days and got the same answer. The therapist was male, appeared young, had only been practicing for four years, and was denied by me because of what I assessed to be perceived hindrances to my therapeutic relationship. However, I was willing to trust my intuition above any and all misplaced belief systems.

I sent him a message to set up a consultation. His response was near immediate. (*Check*.) He did virtual sessions, which allowed me to be in my own safe space while I ventured into my locked away mental spaces. (*Check*.) His energy was felt through the virtual screen, and it was soothing, uplifting, and stable. (*Check*). The last thing checked off my list was something I was sure would be challenging to find in a therapist. He is unavailable for sessions (unless it is an emergency) every third week of the month so he can engage in self-care. (*Check!*) My unfounded assumption that it would be arduous attempting to progress with a male therapist had nearly deprived me of the absolute greatest healing relationship ever!

When a healer realizes they, too, need a healer, feelings of being an imposter may creep into the psyche. To counter this attack on self-love, I reminded myself that it is hypocritical to encourage others to seek therapy, do the hard work of soul progression, heal from your traumas, and become a lover of yourself if I was too prideful to do the same. Since removing that misplaced pride, I have been unlocking the doors to the rooms of my mind that are filled with self-doubt, dissociation, guilt, and distrust. As a work in progress, I am still decluttering these areas to make room for more love.

CHAPTER 7 | LOVE FROM BEHIND THE MASK

Our world conditions us to create masks so that outsiders will see us as healthy, vibrant, intelligent, and moral people. These masks are designed to disguise our vulnerabilities, our depression, anxiety, financial illiteracy, traumas, and fears. We cannot forever remain behind these masks. We must be brave and decide to love who we are without the mask, so we can love ourselves from behind the mask. For me, such a concept entails connecting with the painful experiences of the past so I may feel them, learn from them, and engage in the process of healing from them.

As I come to the point of conclusion, I must add words of wisdom others have gleaned from me. I speak a lot and do not always consider my words to be words of wisdom per se. In preparation for writing on enduring wisdom, I asked those closest to me what lessons or pieces of wisdom they had gleaned from me. I wanted to make sure my life was purposeful to others. Here are their words:

"Be yourself. It's OK to make mistakes. [Learn] how to prioritize, how to budget, how to calm yourself, [and] how to become aware of your surroundings." —Angel White

"Not everything comes your way. Go towards it (work hard). There is both good karma *and* bad karma. When you clean your room (organize), you can find things. Always be prepared—have a backup plan. Don't give people a reason to say negative things; give them a reason to say positive things. Season your food." —Jaden White

ENDURING WISDOM

"Be patient with your healing. Abuse is abuse. Don't expect other people to act the same as you do. You are not everybody's therapist. You don't owe everyone an explanation. It's not your job to save everyone. Take responsibility for your own life. Depression equals constant past reflection. Anxiety equals constant future reflection. Be present." —Jacqueline Green

"Take time to meditate. The beach is a healing source. Listen to what is said, not to respond."

—Dominic Bowman

"Even when life's decisions are the unimaginable, one still has an obligation to do the *noble* thing for the greater good. Everyone has trauma. Some merely mask it better; others simply never believe it exists." —Charles Wood

May you embrace the wisdom of building the courage to love yourself as you live from behind the masks of life. May you realize your genuine value and find yourself worthy of investing in, for it is then that you will prioritize the time and effort needed to grow to your fullest potential. I send you P.E.A.C.E. (Pure Energy and Creative Empowerment) on this journey.

Chapter Eight

It's Start Time: Fully Living through Life's Worst Fears
By Donna Kiel

Donna Kiel

Donna Kiel is an activist, writer, and lover of spontaneous dancing and laughing. Donna is actively reforming her workaholic ways while continuing to help others find passion and purpose in life. She is a life coach, speaker, executive coach, professor, and mentor. Donna has inspired thousands in gaining self-awareness and achieving greater levels of personal and professional success. Her expertise in personal growth combined with educational theory and genuine compassion results in the unique ability to see in others what they may not see in themselves. She holds three degrees, including a BA in psychology, an MA in counseling, and a doctorate in leadership. Donna's specialties include life change, career success, personal fulfillment, anxiety reduction, confident public speaking, and aging with vitality. Donna works with individuals and groups. Donna offers free assessment and consultation for those seeking growth.

She can be reached at

drdonnakiel@gmail.com

or through her website at

www.donnakiel.com.

It's Start Time: Fully Living through Life's Worst Fears

By Donna Kiel

It started with feeling like I was drooling as I walked around masked during COVID-19. That was in April of 2021. The global pandemic of 2020 and 2021 had been in full swing for over a year, and I had thought things were shifting for the better. The onset of the pandemic sent me diving deep into a spiral of fears. Fear consumed me and motivated frantic searches for masks, cleaning supplies, and any form of protection. Though fear raged through my being and consumed my body with constant tightness, sweaty palms, and rapid heartbeat, no one would ever know. You see, I am someone who people typically find reassuring, calm and the source of guidance about fear. I teach others how to remain calm in life. As a professor and as a person, I am the one to come to when things are upended. Yet, here I was, scared beyond any consolation and keeping it a secret.

I did all the things to keep myself and my family safe. I snagged cases of disinfectant, hoarded masks, and coveted all available Lysol wipes. I distanced and stayed locked down. Beyond the fear of COVID, I was consumed with worry that I would lose my job with the millions who lost their jobs. I feared a loss of income and purpose. I became one huge panic attack. I more than panicked; I flipped out.

CHAPTER 8 | IT'S START TIME

Whenever I panic, I must do something. I must find a way to get rid of the pain. You see, I am a master at avoiding pain. My solution to flipping out this time was to kick into overdrive. I had to produce. I had to prove that I was irreplaceable at work. I had to be the one who would ease the angst of all the people suffering from fear while keeping my fear hidden. I started working harder than I ever have in my life. As a professor, I revamped all my classes. I volunteered to help other professors learn how to teach online since it was one of many skills I had. I created new programs that the college could sell. I created a program titled Calm which offered strategies for teachers to help ease their anxiety about teaching online. I created programs to help teachers know how to navigate the challenges of teaching remotely. I was a tornado of work tearing through every problem in education presented by COVID by offering some type of solution that put me at the center of Zoom with others. I was running as fast as I could from my fears by distracting myself with 16-hour workdays. My days became endless Zoom meetings, with my evenings focused on creating programs. I didn't sleep much, and working out (my previous haven) had become limited.

Before COVID, I watched my 1-year-old granddaughter two days a week. Those days were my haven of relief from pre-COVID busy work life. I counted on those days as the break. At the onset of COVID, my daughter decided to stop my visits to keep us all safe. We settled on FaceTime calls with her in the evening. I created special YouTube videos for her to watch so she wouldn't forget me. I went into full production with puppets and books to engage and entertain.

After about five weeks of lockdown, when it looked like the end was not in sight, we decided we could go back to carefully letting me watch her. It broke my heart that she had forgotten me a bit. It took a while for her to warm back up to me. Now, I added watching my granddaughter two days a week with jam-packed workdays. I would fervently work during my granddaughter's naps, and I could attempt to check email in between playing with her as my mind was in a constant state of distraction. Life was this ongoing nightmare of work, hidden anxiety, constant to-do lists, and isolation.

The murder of George Floyd shifted the world and shifted me. It was too much. I had to do something. I also had to keep moving. I created a racial equity program and invited two African American women who I deeply admire and cherish to help me teach the program. I spent endless hours learning, listening, and trying to design learning experiences to address the challenging and complex issues of racism. I coached teachers and principals on the challenges of anti-racism. My days were endlessly filled with a focus on everything but myself. I spent so many hours sitting at my computer that my Apple Watch gave up telling me to stand.

Then, in October of 2020, I noticed my hair shedding more than usual. A FaceTime visit to my doctor indicated stress and the need for blood tests. All the tests came back normal except for the hormone indicators. I desperately needed medication to rectify. I was relieved to know it was a problem that could be medicated. So, despite the doctor's guidance to ease back on the work, to take frequent breaks, to roll out my back in between meetings, I slipped right

CHAPTER 8 | IT'S START TIME

back into the safety of total distraction with work. I was like a drug addict who couldn't live without the fix of 20-hour workdays. My family told me to stop working so hard, my friends told me to stop, my therapist kept attempting strategies—nothing worked. I was gone. Work addiction is a complex issue. The cultural support to work hard makes even seeing the addiction difficult. I became a workaholic to hide from the pain and anxiety I was feeling.

The pandemic and endemic of racism were not only causing me great anxiety and sorrow, but they were causing me to lose myself. I didn't know how to take care of myself anymore. I didn't know who I was without my work. My brief moments of joy with family or friends were distracted by phone checking and trying to always catch up to work. I was gone. Amid the global pandemic, racial reckoning, the divisiveness of our nation, and a transforming world, I lost my love of self. My life pre-pandemic had been rather fragile. As a highly introverted woman who has gone through significant trauma, I had become a master of hiding the scars with a façade of teaching everything I needed to learn. I became my professional role as a teacher of emotional wellness. I was Dr. Kiel, the one who managed a million things with creative ease. In the pandemic, I was Dr. Kiel, who was not only managing a million things but who was working harder than humanly possible. Something had to break.

In May of 2021, the end of the pandemic was near. I had become fully vaccinated in March. I wasn't sure why I didn't feel more joy. It was in April when I noticed the drooling. On May 24, 2021, I had a FaceTime visit with my doctor. She listened as I described a swelling under my right ear—the place where 30 years earlier, I had a tumor removed. She ordered a CT scan and recommended an ENT specialist. She told me to tell her immediately if anything changed. On Thursday, May 27, during a work Zoom call, I thought my face felt numb. I panicked. I could feel my heart race. I ended the meeting by just clicking off without explanation. That is one of the best things about Zoom is you can just click off. I called my doctor. She said to go to the emergency room. I spent what felt like an eternity of 11 hours waiting in the emergency room. I got the CT and an MRI. The emergency room doctors said I had a tumor on my salivary gland. That is what I had 30 years ago. My heart sank, and fear crushed the air out of my chest. Friday, May 28, I talked to my doctor. She went through the labs. I had read them. The wonder of technology truly is not good for someone with anxiety. Seeing all your lab reports on your computer screen is this feeling of drowning in fear and confusion. Add to that, Dr. Google, and you have a recipe for a nervous breakdown.

I told my doctor how frightened I was. I stopped hiding behind this competent, Dr. Kiel, that I had often used. I was petrified and let it be known. She suggested I go for bloodwork that day and then come to see her Monday for pre-op. She said the tumor had to come out. I begged for an earlier appointment with the ENT as the one I had was 10 days later. I couldn't imagine keeping the fear and anxiety inside for 10 days. She said she would try. She texted me no luck on the earlier appointment. I would go in for a pre-op physical on June 1 and wait until June 7 to meet the surgeon. Nothing in this world would be within my control. I was no longer in charge. I'd need to figure out who I was

CHAPTER 8 | IT'S START TIME

without work and within a life-threatening situation and all while trying to figure out how to navigate this fear.

There is the image we project into the world of who we are, and then there is the truth. We all have, as Glennon Doyle calls it, a representative who is our culturally acceptable self. Ideally, we have our representative who shows up when needed, and then we have our true self who we know is our grounded, authentic, and transparent self that we embrace and love. I had lost my true self. There were glimmers of her when I would be playing with my granddaughter. But now, after reading a very tragic Google search result on my tumor, I was demolished. I was very painfully at that breaking point that comes when you see the truth. I was not living. I was just doing. I had become a human worker rather than a human being. I had become addicted to work to cover the deep pain of losing myself. Now, I was consumed with fear and anxiety—the worst fear and anxiety. Fear that I was going to die. There was no more time to hide. There was no time to wait. I could no longer wait for breaks to start living my life and speaking my truth. All the secrets and shame I held inside. All the stories of betrayal, abuse, scandal, and lies needed to be spoken. My voice needed and deserved to be heard.

In a panicked call with my therapist, in which I was asking how I could get through the days of suffocating anxiety, my therapist asked me, "what is the anxiety trying to tell you?" My anxiety was not saying to be afraid of dying. My anxiety was saying, "it's start time." It is time to start living. My anxiety was saying, "stop hiding." My anxiety, my fear, my shame was telling me that I truly do love me. Anxiety is loving something so much it frightens you to lose it. I had consumed myself with work and lost track of me. Yet, the work had changed me. It had shown me all that I can be. Along the way of constantly giving to others, I had grown to love me, and my life. Anxiety was telling me to step into life and start living.

Though as I write this, I have no idea the prognosis of my medical issue, I do know how to navigate the fear and anxiety. My fear has been my greatest wisdom teacher. None of us knows the answer to when or how we will leave this earth. It seems cliché to say all we have is now, but it is all we have. There is no waiting, no start time in the future, no time to get through this so that we can start. I've been waiting all my life to start living. I've been keeping the secrets of all the truths that brought me here as a woman hiding from life. It's time to take the hand of fear and walk out into the open. Fully living through fear happens when we listen to the message. Fear, pain, suffering is our teacher. My fear is telling me to choose me, to speak the truth, to laugh, to find the fun, and to start now.

We are all bundles of fear. It is only when we rest, when we create, when we laugh, and allow play into our lives that we truly live. My anxiety was here to teach me that I am not a worker—work is not my destiny. I am a writer. I am a creator. I am divinely me. You are divinely you. If anything has you afraid right now, if you are a tornado of anxiety of any kind, stop—rest, feel your feet on the floor. Listen to the sounds in the room. Don't run from fear but rather embrace it. Share it. Allow it. Thoughts, after all, are not real unless we let them be real. Ask your anxiety what it is here to teach you. When I ask mine, it is telling me that it is time to start being me, the real me. The greatest

CHAPTER 8 | IT'S START TIME

wisdom I will ever know was hidden inside this fear. My fear was trying to tell me I was on the wrong path. Life is not about how much you do, the titles that you hold, the degrees you attain, or the books you publish. Life is about doing what you love, creating what you want, being in your truth, and it is about love. I have found life in the deep love I have with all those around me. That is my joy. The greatest of those loves is the love I have for me. My fear has served me well in my life. It has kept me safe. It has gotten me good-paying jobs. And this time, it has saved me from losing my path. Turn to your fear—see your goodness—you are there!

Chapter Nine

Finding My Happy
By Amy I. King

Amy I. King

Amy I King is a Certified Life Coach/owner of Your Phenomenal Life, LLC. She taught Social Sciences in public education for a decade. She is a contributing author of international bestsellers: Inspirations: 101 Uplifting Stories for Daily Happiness, Manifestations: True Stories of Bringing the Imagined into Reality, The Grateful Soul: The Art and Practice of Gratitude, The Courageous Heart: Finding Strength in Difficult Times, and Ordinary Oneness: The Simplicity of Everyday Love, Grace and Hope.

When not writing, she enjoys music, movies, art, travel, new adventures and challenges, spending time with animals, connecting with the natural world around us and time with loved ones.

Amy has overcome a plethora of challenges, including Spina bifida, narcissistic abuse, cancer, and loss from which she draws wisdom to assist clients. Amy's greatest joy is using her personal experiences to help others move past their personal blocks and outdated beliefs to becoming empowered to live the life of their dreams. Every challenge, she believes, is put before us to help us to evolve and grow into the greatest version of ourselves. She loves to help people discover and step into the best version of themselves. If you have a dream for a better life, Amy would love to help you.

Her relationships with clients are built on trust and vulnerability. She is currently coaching and writing her first solo book, Messy Wheels: Stories from Where I Sit, available on Amazon in 2021. She welcomes the opportunity to work with you to help you transform your life into the phenomenal one that you deserve!

yourphenomenallife585@gmail.com

or (916) 718-0914 text/call.

Finding My Happy
By Amy I King

Driving up the highway toward home, after a fantastic week with friends who are more like family, I realize something. I am happy. You may be thinking to yourself, well yeah. However, it has taken a lot of time and effort to get there. I was raised to be good, work hard, put on a false front that everything is lovely, and fit an image. I didn't know how to be happy. The importance of happiness didn't reveal itself to me until quite a few years after my mother gave me the sage advice to "Be happy" on her proverbial death bed. It would be years before I even gave it a thought.

I look down at my soap-lathered leg, propped up on the bench, ready to be shaved. My eyes go to the words "Be Happy" tattooed on my leg as part of a tribute to my mother. The day that she passed, we had expected her to be well enough to come home with us—just the day before, she had shown vast improvement. I arrived at the hospital early in the morning only to be intercepted by the doctor who had been in charge of my mother's case. She had been diagnosed with ALS two years earlier and was in the ICU with a respiratory infection. "Your mom is going to need to be on the Bi-PAP 24 hours a day for breathing," she said. Her decline was a huge blow. My mother had been doing well throughout her two-year diagnosis of ALS with breathing, despite losing her ability to walk. I was devastated.

CHAPTER 9 | FINDING MY HAPPY

The doctor asked if I wanted her to speak with my mom. I said, "I'll tell her." I went into my mom's hospital room, took her hand, and I got the words out without crying. My mother chose to go that day. An adventurous spirit, she was not the type of person who would have done well tied to a machine. Our small family gathered, we played music, and we had our last conversations, one by one. That last conversation with my mother was one I will cherish forever. We said the things we needed to say, cleaned up some mess, and ended in a great space. She imparted some wisdom to me that day when she stated, "Be happy." My response was that I would try. She said, "No, be happy."

Five years passed when I received the text, "I'll leave you alone." It came from the remaining member of my family of origin. The text responded to my request that the focus shift from illness to wellness, as I had to keep moving forward. That was December 2018, one of the lowest points in my life. In July of that year, I lost my grandmother, and then in November, I was diagnosed with breast cancer in my left breast. I had a lumpectomy to remove cancer and then went on immunotherapy. Alone and spent, I was in survival mode. Happiness was the furthest thing from my mind at that moment, but my mother's words on her deathbed rang out. "Be happy." I was far from happy. I was lost, alone, untethered. I felt like an empty vessel. I cried for days as I sat in misery. And then I made a decision. I was going to honor my mother's last directive. I was going to be happy. I began to say yes to the things that resonated with me. It was my goal to be happy.

An event called The International Women's Summit was being advertised all over the Internet. I believe in the nudges, so it was clear to me that attending was in my future. I bought a VIP ticket to the event for myself, a first-class plane ticket, and booked a room. I thought, "Why not? Life is short, and I am traveling alone." I might as well do it right. Attending the event changed my life. I went into it with an open mind and an even more open heart. I was not alone for long. I found my soul tribe of lovely, powerful women, and I had found a publisher. Writing and becoming a published author had been a goal for years. Now I had the how. It was all within reach, and I was ready to grab on.

At home, I had a bathroom that wasn't genuinely accessible. I've used a wheelchair for the past 20 years and have always adapted to my environment. I had been living in my home as though I were a guest. I could not treat myself so poorly any longer. After living here for seven years, I decided it was time to honor myself with a bathroom that worked for me.

I moved into a hotel the week after returning from the Women's Summit, and renovation began. While living in the hotel, a friend and I attended a comedy show and a concert. My cheeks hurt from smiling after both events. Life and everything that it had to offer was now a huge priority.

I also began to heal on the inside. Years and years of pain, resentment, anger, fear, feelings of rejection and loneliness were piled up inside of me. I healed childhood scars of which I had not even been cognizant. Guttural cries erupted from within my body. This sure as heck wasn't happy, but maybe it was leading to it. The healing went on, the crying

CHAPTER 9 | FINDING MY HAPPY

continued, and then one day, I realized that I was getting to the center of the onion. You see, when you are healing, you are akin to an onion. The layers peel away slowly, revealing more pain in need of healing. Some of the pain will surprise you, as you didn't even know it was there. Other pain will be obvious. It is not a pleasant process, but it is well worth doing the hard work of healing. Every time you heal a little, you feel a bit lighter.

Many changes have come about as a result of doing the work. Many of my friendships have deepened and become much more honest, and some of my friendships have ended. And that is ok! I realized that I was holding on to people for the sake of having people. That was my fear in action. I had lost so many family members to death in such a short period that I was holding on for dear life. I have learned that the quality of your relationships is an indicator of the quality of your life. So, cleaning house and getting my relationships in order was a necessary step on the road to happiness. The friendships I have today are sincere. If someone is having a bad day, we talk about it. If there is conflict in the relationship, we talk about it. Those who refuse to own their stuff are not welcome. Arriving at this boundary was not easy, and I didn't take it lightly. However, some people will get angry with you when you call them on their stuff. Those aren't your people. My friends can call me on my stuff all day long, and I am willing to self-evaluate and course-correct if needed. And that goes both ways.

Self-care has become an essential part of my life. Exercising, eating right, sleep, getting enough sunshine, meditation, communing with nature, practicing gratitude, and spending time with the people who I value all have a place of importance in my life. I roll down the street in my wheelchair, about two miles each day. There are mornings I wake up and do not want to exercise. But, I begrudgingly put in my earbuds and head out the door, usually with a podcast keeping me company. Moving my body keeps me clear and is helping me to lose the Covid weight. Yes, I put on weight during the lockdown. And I'm not too happy about it. Instead of wallowing in the misery, I am doing something about it. Exercise is beneficial in a variety of ways. The obvious being that it helps us to lose weight. It also clears the mind of a lot of the gunk. It assists with creativity and with your overall sense of self. It boosts confidence and gets you out of your head. Most importantly, it increases mood. It makes you feel happier.

Eating right has been a massive shift for me. Learning that I was gluten sensitive, I removed it from my diet. I also removed dairy. My digestive system thanked me! I was no longer suffering from bloating and diarrhea. Gross, I know! But, guess what? When you began eating better, your body feels better. That is something about which to be happy.

I got on a regular sleep schedule and noticed that I could sleep for 8 hours on a good program. The contribution to my mood and overall feeling of well-being was priceless. Sleep is vital and necessary. Without it, we are zombies.

I began spending more time outside. Meditation is an integral part of my daily life, and I love to be outdoors. So, I figured why not kill two birds with one stone? Now, I take the time to go out, weather permitting, sit quietly and meditate every day. It works to ground and center the mind

CHAPTER 9 | FINDING MY HAPPY

and brings me a great sense of inner peace. I recommend trying it if you are open. You might be surprised by the difference it makes.

Sunshine is a natural mood booster. No one can be miserable when the sun is shining down on them. Ok, maybe some people can! For the most part, when we are in the sunshine, we are happy humans! And while you are out there, try touching some plants. Gardening is an act of self-love. Get your hands in that dirt and feel the earth! Those happy feelings are waiting for you!

Get out there in nature. Explore and witness the majesty of it all. I am very fortunate to live in a place where I don't have to go far to find it. I can go out on my back patio, and I am on a veritable nature preserve. The hummingbird family who lives in my tree—the turkey trio will respond to a whistle with a few gobbles. I've seen the occasional coyote and skunk, as well. The other day, I returned home from a road trip to Southern California. I was outside returning the hummingbird feeder to its post. I turned around in time to witness an enormous lizard making its way into my home over the hump of the sliding glass door track. My first thought was, "Oh, no, how am I going to get this creature to leave?" I said, as sweetly as I could, "Come back outside," as though he knows English! Then, I watched as he entered, sat for a moment, and then came back outside. He left me a little package in a puddle, if you know what I mean. Ew. I love nature.

Realizing that we are all connected has been an extraordinary shift.

Practicing gratitude has shifted my perspective in ways I never imagined. Writing that list every morning puts me in a frame of mind that is positive and ready to take on the day. When we are in a space of gratitude, we are open to an abundance of people and situations for which to be grateful.

Connecting with people who feed my soul is an important practice. Whether by phone or meeting for lunch, I find that my connections to those I love makes me happy. My friends are family and those relationships are priceless.

Learning how to put me first has been one of the biggest hurdles I have experienced on this journey to happiness. In the past, the needs of others were always more important to me than my own needs. I learned to be a fixer. If there was a problem, I was there to solve it, even to my detriment. I would loan someone money when I had bills to pay. I had to stop that if I was ever going to be happy. I have learned that there will always be someone ready to take advantage of your generosity. Be generous with yourself first. I have had "friends" who have told me their sob stories because they know that I will be there to help them. Those people are not your friends. Those are people who like to use others for their benefit.

Stop putting yourself last, I had to tell myself. I cannot tell you how many of those people I attracted in the past; I can tell you that I am no longer attracted to users. I attract into my life people who bring with them love, joy, honesty, and a sense of loyalty, and the ability to take care of themselves. I can tell the people in my circle anything without fear of abandonment. When you say to a user no, they leave. I know; we don't want users in our lives. But,

CHAPTER 9 | FINDING MY HAPPY

the old me was holding on to those very people. Learning to discern between a friend and a user has been one of the best things to come from my healing process. I have a circle that is honest, loving, supportive, uplifting, positive, and authentic. There is no-thing fake.

We must learn healthy boundaries to be truly happy. Years ago, when someone would present an opportunity, my knee-jerk reaction was an immediate yes. Now, when presented with a request for my time or anything else, I sit in quiet contemplation. The reply is not prompt. Depending on the situation, it may take a couple of days to get back to someone. If it resonates with me, I will say yes. If not, it's a clear no. Boundaries have been a complicated thing for me to understand and implement. Some of my family members did not respect my boundaries as I was growing up. Told who I was; a grossly inaccurate character depiction was thrust upon me by the narcissist in the family. It turns out I was not that person at all. I am who I decide I am. And that is a strong, intelligent, independent, loving, resilient, aware, joy-filled, boundary respecting, nature-loving, fantastic friend to those who are deserving. I am a lover of life and all that it has to offer.

Happiness is ultimately the result of a multitude of decisions. We can wallow in misery or dust ourselves off and deal with the challenges life throws our way. There is always a choice. Happiness is an inside job. Get to the core of who you are, and you will find your happiness.

Mom, I can honestly say that after all of the pain and trauma that I have worked through,

I am happy.

Chapter Ten

Generational Perspective
By Geneva Dantes

Geneva Dantes

Born on Bunker Hill Day, celebrating when hope is found in defeat. This explains my optimism and desire to keep moving forward, always with the knowing that the day might be cloudy, but the sun is always present. A screaming left brain that loves order and fairness, with a right brain whispering, be creative; the path leads me to help others. To find order in chaos as I gently nudge for happiness. My grateful thanks to the high school teacher who was certain, everyone has a book to write. To the college professor who found my poems to be the best. And to Dr. Wayne Dyer who advised us not to die with your music still in you. Keep moving, keep striving to understand. Have a blessed day.

GenevaDantes11@gmail.com

Generational Perspective
By Geneva Dantes

What is the path, the steps are dark, who holds the light? What do you gain from being here? So many speak, seldom hear the truth to whom the listener dwells. Pause the thought, what remains for you to sing, to soar, to exist. Ponder, realize, know delusions left alone. Generations speak to you and hold the light to seek.

Remember your perfect picture. Before you were but always are, you have the great design. All function in your own pattern, unique is what it is. For this trip that may be, but yours to choose or change. For all was thought has turned somehow, the perfect being is called. To summon forth the need is immense. The time is now to look deep. To what was, to what will be, to those called to assist. You may not recall the help brought with you, the design in place. By you and to you, the wisdom to grow, to know, to share. All who share are here with you, but to pause, to listen, to know.

What each should teach to one who learns. What is seen as strife, the burden at your request. Breath deep to know, support is here in many forms, though some seem bitter. The taste to know and not to share, tears that wash others clean. You have strength when they do not. Tears drawn by those who help, yet difficult to see. Why one succeeds, the other fails, consider which is true. Truth soars within, transcends it all.

CHAPTER 10 | GENERATIONAL PERSPECTIVE

Who Creates

Who creates what is true? Your truth, their truth, reality unknown. Set the base, build the form, where you chose to grow. You own not the reality of others; universes in opposition yet parallel. What tools are given; what tools withheld, the clothes you wear set the stage. A mind confused, no sense is found, a child is left alone. To suffer with love unknown and seek to find a meaning. It is sorrow in this place for you to understand, no help from others, unkind you see. No hand to help the seed. Water given is brown, soil rocky, but the sky above is blue. Your only help to survive, within you always is. To reach out is to disappoint, understand your path, your motive, your way. They help you not, yet together you grow. It is difficult to understand, remember well, that is your plan.

Be not manipulated by obligation and fear. This a lesson to learn. What you see and what you are, is only to survive. Keep others happy to save yourself, look to test what is so. Is this lovely, is this true, is the happiness for you? A desperate life to live in fear and keep well by giving away, all you have and all you are to those who take away. You cannot see, you cannot stop all waves roll to take. They are happy, for a moment you rest. Small stillness to breath to find nothing left. You strive to be more, to give more, to lose more and do not see. They take because you give.

Even in your dreams you wander lost and know not the way. You look for meaning but left confused by night and by day. The circle you do not see. Another hill another turn; how can that be? You just were here, the path has changed, though you turn around to see. What went wrong, why this place unchanged by steps well planned and trod. Confusion stares back at you. You breath, you step, you look around. What next, what more, what was missed. You do not understand. To sleep, to dream, to be awake to hear the distant call.

Who Protects

Who protects in this time? Give an inch to get a mile, selfless not in deed. Manipulate the ones around to your liking be. Not the good, not the wise though wisdom is what you see. Not is true, you fool yourself to thinking blessing come. You have it now but what the cost to those whose trust you wain. For in your heart not satisfied the empty place to fill. The things to get, no love they bring, no peace, quietly you sigh.

There are those who long to please, when in your presence be. To see you smile, to avoid the pain of what displeases you. Your wrath avoid, the price is high for meek a burden to bare. Who turns to you for wisdom sought or mere happiness to find? Comfort there to you they turn seeking what do they find? The emptiness, the thick façade for they want you to be. Want and wanted the blend is difficult to see. Confusion reigns, who are you, to the world you long.

The chameleon blends to fit with all, to be part of something small. The best in you stands tall and true. Tell yourself and you do. Hush the noise that frightens you, be the aspect you are. Give what is yours to give, take not what others have. For what they have is part of them and not part of you. Yours is yours to offer all, you are special, you are part, but not of that which is tiny. For in your eyes,

CHAPTER 10 | GENERATIONAL PERSPECTIVE

focus to see what you bring to support eternity. Peace is within and smile at them who do not share your path. We all arrive, we find truth, make your path your own. For others' travels may shine bright, but nothing so is true. Love the you, embrace yourself for what protrudes remains. Not to the left. Not to the right, in the center stay. Focus what is in front of you, the here the now the present that is. Ruminate not, the story past, in the moment reveal your best; in harmony we sing.

Who Tests

Who tests the plan; what is yours to take, what is yours to give, knowing is the secret. Fooled again, the tear is shed and rolls past your cheek, the smile that fades. Here you droop and wonder why, which turn should be taken. To stop this mill, this circle not still, but runs without fruition. The cost today, the benefits weigh the certainty of the picture. The whole obscured by random fear to fill the gap today. But when today ends tomorrow, what in your hand you hold? Your heart knows truth and shall prevail amid the chaos now.

Emotions communicate, a sound to be heard. The noise within, the mirror without. What do you see? Feel your feelings, allow emotions to shriek. In that voice hasten to hear the sound of truth, the song of fear. Give voice a chance to flow to reach the waterfall. Cascade feel free and gather with those who await see you rise closer to destiny. Your quiet mind in stillness knows, relax, breath in, let it flow past the tone stuck in time.

Give, love, and happiness, doing what is true. Life itself repeat; all has been before. The obstacle in front of you, what you chose before. To look again and understand nonsense for you to see. To see it now and know the truth of what is best for you. To help another is surely just but know the price you pay. What greater good befits you here what part are you to play? Who is the victim in this case, who is saving whom? To know the difference to see both sides is what you need to do. Go forth with this, correct the past in the present now. When all is good no sadness stays for love has done its best. Know this is true and walk away, accept was is meant to be. Do not look back or linger here or in that place you stay. Though you know the deed is done, the price you pay no more. No others do the work for them, they themselves must see, the burden not yours to bare. You did your best, you offered all, now their choice, their path to walk alone.

Who Grows

Who grows, springs forth? When words escape that angry place, react to your day in an angry way. Forgive them, forgive yourself, move forward. Do not look back to contemplate the moment to view no more. What was spoken, what was done, was the breath exhaled. Mistakes in others apply to you, your memory intact. What you see in them, you may avoid, their lesson you may learn. Your heart is true to see that path, avoid the cause to others. Diminish sorrow, shame, and hate the path known not taken.

CHAPTER 10 | GENERATIONAL PERSPECTIVE

Learning and growing are for tomorrow, if today you morn. Sadness comes and sits with you for what you see no more. The feeling has not adjusted. To what was then and was is now the corner is to turn. Time it takes, pace yourself, leave none of it behind. It follows you and scare your night until blessed and let go. Shadows linger not in light.

Breathe in again bring in light, know yourself is true. Some rain will fall, winds blow harsh, dust gets in your eyes. Brush away, dry your face, pick up to meet the day. Each one is new another turn to practice what shines. Smile deep inside, it is in you still, compassionately free.

Who Supports

Who supports your plan; this the treasure you seek to find? The help for you to know. To understand what others share, to find the wisdom there. You must seek, you must hear to grasp the mix the timing of your plan. If all at once you cannot carry and take all with you. Share not your joy with those who laugh, they do not understand.

Again you judged, your feelings hurt for kindness you expected. What was found, what was share disappointed. Not your place, not your time, consider when lounging there. Want, hope, expecting support not seen. Take joy, add fear, subtract that hope, and multiply by too many. Look again, look past desire and perhaps another will fill. What drew you here to your surprise, pleasant if you look. With different eyes observe the course, the players you understand. Which outcome did you seek?

Stand for yourself, assert your needs. Express with confidences, a vortex of dignity. Lift up the boot, intend, move, more hope and try again. The Universe is one with all, remember you are one. Though the path in front is blurred, backward is not for you. Solve the riddle, repeating is slow and stuck. Court the solution, not material objects you seek; acceptance, appreciation, acknowledgment to feel. Things are things, what you know is dear.

When all is glum and nothing done, your day stands ill. Hush to see the will, the longing to survive. When days are dark and shadows loom, recall the sun, the sand, the sea. Waves roll in and gently nudge you to the shore to rest. Still waves roll in and waves roll out, but for a moment of ease. Take solace here to reflect, gather new a plan. Look across the waters, they beckon you to see the changing choice. All is up, all is down, the movement is consistent. Some ride the wave, some fall under, but the shore they always reach. They catch their breath and go again to heed a distant voice. This voice you know, the sound is sweet, in your heart you know. Exhale the sad, inhale the love. The call is there, you go again, it is what you take with you. Remember them, they are with you in the ocean vast. Sometimes you meet, sometimes pass, sometimes you ride together.

Who Loves

Who reveals love without knowing, touches your heart, how does it beat? A moment of love to see. The moment that brings you life with hope, now possibilities see. Your chance to nurture love, be the foundation strong. You know

CHAPTER 10 | GENERATIONAL PERSPECTIVE

the pain, you set aside, that which you do not share. To one so small, to one so sweet, only love you give. Recall the feeling, it does exist. Breathe and take it in.

Held in your arms, what you have, what do you create? The sorrow, the hate, the emptiness, not to enter here. For what you have, for what you are, is what you take with you. The love, the joy, bring peace to life. For what it is, for what it was, for what it will always be. You create, it is what you are, the love for all to see.

The window of time, the cradle of life, differences appear. Happy, glad, the cranky one whose life begins with pain. In the moment you pause, when all is still, eternity recalled. The good in all, a time to glimpse, remember well my friend. The flood of love you become, even for a moment glimmer. Embrace it all, the whole of life beyond the pain expand.

Your past is fear, your future dread, but in that moment smile. When darkness looms, choose new beliefs. Your past is clear, your future bright, in this moment smile. External hollow, find inner peace. Be the light illuminate, forgiveness does prevail. What you create, what grow next, shine love and nurture well; know joy, know peace, know happiness.

Share your wisdom, help others grow, not a manifesto for life. Word for now, words for later, words from your past. All are one, each person, one generation is now. Not each is all, not a basket or box, a piece is here a part is there. Learn which to choose, to give and take, each has good, each has bad, your wisdom emerges to see. How to choose, how to accept a peaceful pursuit of blessedness.

The good, the bad, the sum of things, is what you decide to see. The good, the bad, the sum of things is what you decide to be. For what you were, for what you are, for what you will always be. You might be small, but what is size, a whisper touches hearts. To a stranger on a train a random gift indeed. To observe, not to judge, allow your words to speak. Pursue the path which you desire, your heart sings. You celebrate with no one watching, care not if they do.

The more the path, the light to shine, shared throughout the ages. Do not be dim, no not hide, be the ray of light. From generations passed and generations to be; guide the way for other who stray and fumble in the dark. Grow past your thoughts, open to another, walk the path, light the way.

Chapter Eleven

Speaking Stones
By Becki Koon

Becki Koon

Becki Koon is a Heart-based Energy Intuitive, Reiki Master, HeartMath Coach, Life Coach, Crystal Practitioner, and Author/Speaker. Through her business, Step Stone, Becki empowers people to seek their inner wisdom while holding space for them to heal, discover, and grow into the next highest version of themselves. She likes to refer to herself as the mid-wife of birthing a person's remembrance of their divine essence or purpose.

Becki has a passion to share energy awareness with those seeking a new way to experience their realities. The recent loss of her husband opened her up to an even deeper level of acceptance, love, and gratitude. Becki and Jack shared a common love of crystals and stones. The business they created is full of the stones and crystals they personally gathered, as well as stones that magically found their way to them. They recognized the use of stones as an integral part of the conscious death journey Jack took in 2019.

While Becki's background is broad, all of her experiences have a common thread—her passion for helping people, the land, animals, and the community through heart-centered, compassionate action. Becki believes in the interconnectedness of all things. She says, "I have come to embrace there are three aspects to the person I am: 1) coming from heart-centered action, 2) communicating with integrity to the best of my ability, and 3) having vision to see the incredible potential in all beings on and off the planet.

"I am excited to be part of bringing Spiritual Ecology, Unity Consciousness, Stone and Crystal Energetic Partnership, and Spirit Connection to the forefront of conscious awareness in the mass population."

stepstone2you@gmail.com
www.beckikoon.com
www.facebook.com/becki.koon.consulting
amazon.com/author/beckikoon
Phone (406) 360-2211

Speaking Stones
By Becki Koon

I'm having a hard time relaxing, thinking I will not be able to 'see' into the stone that has called me to meditation. I feel into the still moment when—whoosh—down into the rock I go as if pulled by a magical force. I find myself in a massive cavern that echoes with the reverberation of my breath. I feel an energy buzz penetrating all of my cells, signaling alertness in my awareness. I gaze upon huge, crystal-clear quartz columns and stalactites that shimmer with rich, iridescent colors like a magical rainbow. The light in the cavern is ethereal, from an unknown source. I say hello a few times and hear my voice echo, echo, echo into the vastness of the space. I feel my body melt into the experience of being held in divine love, a familiar feeling of 'knowing' the comfort of Earth's womb, the living, breathing Gaia. I am one with her.

The stone I am inside of speaks. "I have recently been unearthed from the bowels of the Mother. I am of the granite family. It is no accident you found me pointing towards the root system of a tree. I break off small pieces of myself to nourish the tree and surrounding plants. The tree I was nourishing has been harvested, so it was time for you to find me. I am here to remind you of your ability to connect and communicate with the stones, the trees, the earth. You have the ability to step into this gift of aware-

CHAPTER 11 | SPEAKING STONES

ness. Do not deny it. Do not deny it. Listen and honor your ability, your God-given gift."

That experience was my journey into the stone, an activity I performed while on a vision quest high in the mountain wilderness of Idaho. Part of my preparation task for making my way on a 3-day solo journey was going into meditation with a stone. I looked around my campsite for a rock that seemed to stand out amongst all the others scattered on the ground. The one that called to me was nondescript, a simple stone of gray and black with a bit of moss on one side. It was pointed towards a tree stump; I had a strong pull, so I trusted the nudge. I picked up the stone, holding it in my hands as I found my way to sit and rest my back against a full-grown pine tree. The scent of the bark helped me drift into stillness, and I then journeyed into the heart of the stone, the crystal womb that engulfed me.

What was this awareness the stone asked me not to deny?

All these years later, I ponder the amazing connection to stones that has carried on throughout my life. What is it about the power of stones and crystals that seems to mesmerize people of all ages?

As a small child, I was intrigued by my dad's rock collection. To this day, my brother and I have a friendly exchange about who gets dad's most beautiful agate, the one that has awe-inspiring purples and pinks swirling in a circle on the exposed surface. (My brother seems to have ended up with this beauty.) I would often find stones to pick up and admire while walking anywhere a stone happened to appear. This activity has never ceased. I walked with my children, admiring and picking up stones to take home or put in my pocket, encouraging them to do the same when it was appropriate.

Some places are sacred, and the stones need to be left, honoring the landscape. It is essential to understand local environmental requirements and use intuition whether to pick up or leave the stone in place. Intuitive insight will give a yes or no response in those who are aware of it. The stone will let them know if it wants to be left behind or to travel with them. It is best to go with the first flash of insight or feeling. I have had stones give me a no response to traveling with me while others are delighted to join me and work with me. I have learned to trust that flash of awareness.

I know it may sound crazy for me to say you can talk to the stones, but this planet is a magical place. We are just now beginning to understand the quantum nature of our world.

I now find myself with granddaughters who have the same fascination with stones and crystals, no different than I at their tender young age. My family is not an anomaly. People have had a fascination with stones and crystals for eons, probably for as long as humans have walked the earth and felt her magic.

Yes, we make shelter and tools with stone. Stone caves kept us from the elements and out of harm's way. Stone was used to chisel drawings and writings during the great

CHAPTER 11 | SPEAKING STONES

civilizations of antiquity. We grind our spices, grains, and wheat with stone mills. We use crystals in our technology: our computers, cell phones, and LED screens. We use stones to build impressive structures, such as homes, churches, roads, bridges, fences; the list goes on ad infinitum. But the connection to stones runs much deeper than the innumerable practical uses we have found in physical form.

For centuries, stones and crystals have been used not only for their utility but also for their energetic properties, beauty, and power. Ancient sacred sites worldwide used stone structures to amplify the power and magic of ceremonies housed within those formations. Stones, gems, and crystals have been worn as talismans, amulets, armor plates, and symbols adorning the body as jewelry.

Jade has been mined in China for at least 6,000 years and has been used for carvings, statues, ceremonial weapons, ritual objects, and jewelry. Jade was used to adorn the grave furnishings of the high-ranking members of Imperial families, and one mummy found was covered from head to toe in a Jade bodysuit. The Chinese believed Jade would bestow immortality and help preserve the body from decaying after death.

In ancient Egypt, stones were used in burial finery to adorn the body. One of the most interesting uses was grinding Lapis Lazuli into a paste for Cleopatra to wear as an eye adornment, much as eye shadows are used by women today. Stones were also ground into powders used for medicinal purposes. The Death Mask of Tutankhamen had beautiful inlays of Lapis Lazuli, Turquoise, Carnelian, and other gems. Lapis was considered to have God-like qualities and symbolized the night sky, life, the heavens, and God. One of the oldest mines in the world, over 7,000 years in production, is the Sar-i-Sang Lapis Lazuli mine in the Badakhshan region of Afghanistan.

Many priests, seers, and dowsers have used crystals and stones for divination and sight into the unknown realms of spirit. The Bible mentions the breastplate of the High Priest of Israel was made of twelve stones of great value, with two shoulder ornament stones offsetting the powerful breastplate configuration. The twelve stones are said to represent the Twelve Tribes of Israel and were considered most precious to the Israelites.

Two well-known stones of divination are called the Urim and Thummim. These stones are first mentioned in the Book of Exodus and are considered an inclusion on the breastplate. The High Priest would use these stones to answer a question or reveal the will of God to the seeker. These stones are mentioned numerous times throughout Christian history as they are associated with cleromancy. Cleromancy is a form of casting of lots, in which an outcome is determined by means that generally would be considered random, such as the rolling of dice, but are believed to reveal the will of God or other universal forces and entities. In the book of Mormon, Joseph Smith was presented with the Urim and Thummim stones which led to his extraordinary visions birthing a religious movement that has grown to be a worldwide organization.

In Druid tradition, the Adder stone was prized for extra-ordinary virtues. The Adder stone is traditionally glassy

CHAPTER 11 | SPEAKING STONES

inside with a naturally occurring hole in the stone. They are also called hag stones or witches stones, depending on the area in which they are used. A more modern version of the Adder stone says that any stone with a hole bored through it by naturally occurring water is considered to hold the energetic virtues the Druids espoused.

These are just a few examples of how effective using stones has been in guiding human development, augmenting and amplifying visions and information shared with humanity. Many other religions and organizations have understood the magical qualities of stones and have used these natural energy conduits to assist them in their work.

Even with all the historical evidence and anecdote, personal experience with stones, gems, and crystals is something of value to many of us as we navigate our world of physical form and energy. My sensitivity to Earth, the living being known as Gaia, started early in life and never faltered. Somehow, I inherently knew the power of working with and being around stones but then again, I am not alone in that awareness.

Thousands of books are written about the energetic properties of stones and crystals. No doubt, those interested can find books that resonate with them, their interests, and their passions of discovery. I would also encourage these people to find their unique connection to the stones. Much like my meditation, I found a direct connection to the stone I held in my hand through my own experience.

Step Stone was the name chosen for my business because I have turned this life-long connection into part of the service I offer, a step stone on the path to someone's self-discovery and healing. As an Empath and Energy Intuitive, crystals have become family members to the energy healing taking place. There are stones scattered throughout the wellness center; all placed intentionally, strategically. A Reiki peace grid is constantly activated with crystals mined from Crystal Park in Montana. Also, a Crystal Light Bar is often placed above the Reiki table for added energetic color and crystal healing. Individual stones and crystals may be placed on a person's body while in session. Stones are used in helping amplify or ground the experience of meditation and connection to the higher realms of awareness. I connect to one of my guides through the use of purple stones, much like a seer uses the stones to view into the realms of spirit. The melding with Gaia energies is profound and a natural part of the evolution of healing and spiritual expansion. The power of having stones and crystals in the healing rooms, the amplification and facilitation of energy movement, are part of the unique energetic field created.

The power of stones became very personal for me when in 2019, my husband and soul mate, Jack, was diagnosed with terminal cancer. I wrote about the journey we took from diagnosis to death in the Amazon best-selling book titled *20 Days Changed Everything, A Love Story: Moving Through Conscious Death to Afterlife Connection*. When we knew it was not about his survival but his passing, we actively participated in sacred activities that helped us both release his physical form to his transition into Spirit. Stones played a considerable role in our epic journey towards the death of his physical body.

We both knew stones carry powerful energetic properties, but we did not necessarily understand all of the nuances

CHAPTER 11 | SPEAKING STONES

each particular stone holds. All we knew was that certain stones carried a powerful energy exchange for Jack. Near his bed, he had me place crystals he had found: the smokey quartz, the recorder quartz, the amethyst I had gifted him; the azurite I found for him while in New Mexico. He had me place his stone necklaces by the photo of me in a Redwoods forest. He wore the ring I had made for him from a beautiful blue agate he found on the Oregon Coast. All of these stones meant something to him, so they were constantly near. We had added selenite and moldavite to the side table as well. The Reiki Peace Grid was stationed nearby.

One stone we had never worked with was Black Kyanite. That stone was gifted to Jack by our Family Nurse Practitioner. She is also a Metaphysician. She handed him the stone as we left her office the day we had a Medical Intuitive session. She looked at Jack with teary eyes, and when he offered to pay for the stone, she said no, it was her gift. She turned to walk away as her emotions began welling up inside. He complimented her and told her what a unique soul she was, how much his work with her had meant to him; he was blessed to know her.

The Black Kyanite meant something beyond our awareness; we did not have time to look it up before I found Jack using it on his solar plexus chakra in a deep meditative state. It did not matter at that moment. What mattered was the powerful energy I felt emanating from his body while a surge moved through me. I was guided to sit next to him and place my hand on his. The words I spoke carried a strength beyond anything I had felt before, and I had a knowing of our eternal journey, a commitment to a greater purpose. Jack and I played out our roles to create a display of divine love for others to see. Jack knew I would be writing about this death walk he was taking, and I was assisting. The bigger picture was ever-present in our minds. In those moments of stepping back from the Becki in physical form to the soul Becki, my suffering and grief were dampened.

When we finished our shamanistic soul empowerment, I looked up the energetic properties of Black Kyanite. I was in awe of the synchronicity of life and the gift of enlightened spiritual tools such as stones.

In Judy Hall's book, *The Crystal Bible 2*, she describes Black Kyanite as "an Earth tool to assist in moving into the between-life state, to access and manifest the current soul plan and release soul imperatives that no longer serve a purpose. This stone shows the karma currently being created by present choices and assists in foreseeing the outcome of a soul plan."

How perfect, the gift for remembering his soul plan and how to leave the physical realm! He courageously left the planet ten days later. Our love of stones never ceased even in his death passage. The depth of sacred power I witnessed with Jack consciously calling his death process forward through sheer spiritual will, without the aid of drugs, is a part of my soul held in the deepest reverence and love. Do I believe the Black Kyanite assisted his rites of passage? I absolutely have no doubt! That stone is now housed in a powerfully blessed location, creating a divine, sacred essence honoring our eternal love.

CHAPTER 11 | SPEAKING STONES

I realize not everyone will have such a strong alliance with stones, but I can almost guarantee most people can feel the life force and power of Earth when they venture into nature. Children automatically want to climb the large boulders they find, put stones in their pockets, and are drawn into the intricacies and colors of even the simple stones. As humans, we are mesmerized by photos we see of massive crystal formations deep within the Earth; caves feel mysterious, and we find ourselves wanting to explore the beauty we see.

I encourage others to take in and experience the *Enduring Wisdom* the planet has to offer. The living Gaia has many magical secrets to share if we choose to explore her multi-dimensional realms. Stones and crystals work with us to provide beauty in our surroundings, create beautiful physical structures, adorn our bodies with powerful support, amplify the sacred energies of ceremony and provide energetic companionship. Please, do not deny the connection!

Chapter Twelve

Meaning Matters, Got Meaning?
By Paula Meyer

Paula Meyer

After becoming a widow at 54, Paula Meyer left her job and began a year of travel to heal her heart. As her travel ended, the Covid-19 pandemic began. The strategies for navigating the grief of her husband's death from throat cancer also helped with the grief from the pandemic and social unrest.

Losing her freedom and lifestyle, she was thrown into the unknown just as her new business began. Her new book, *Great Loss, Greater Love: The Art & Heart of Navigating*

Grief, chronicles her year of travel and is a #1 International Bestseller on Amazon.

Paula has over 30 years of experience as an event planner and contracting specialist, with 12 years in author/speaker management. She has organized and managed 151 workshops around the world. Her company, GP Eventworx, specializes in event production for speaker/teacher workshops, as well as grief retreats for women. She has traveled to 20 countries, some multiple times, and 40 US States. Her goal is to visit 30 countries and all 56 US States and territories by the end of 2025.

Learn more at www.greatlossgreaterlove.com

Meaning Matters, Got Meaning?
By Paula Meyer

As Martha Beck says, "The way we do anything is the way we do everything."

And the "way we do everything" is determined by the meaning that we assign to it. Thus, this famous saying could also be said, "The meaning we give anything is the meaning we give everything."

The way in which we give meaning to things permeates throughout our lives. For me, the belief that I had no voice, that what I had to say was not important, and the very meaning that I gave to those beliefs is what created the energy around what I brought into my life. That belief brought silence within me for many years, in fact, much of my life. It also brought in many people that didn't allow my voice to be heard. And I didn't realize that belief was the culprit for my continued and increasing invisibility for quite a long time, well into my adulthood.

I was watching a movie the other day that was steeped in Catholicism and the idea of confession. As the young student was questioning the purpose of confession, I thought to myself that confession is really just the simple and humble act of speaking your voice, your hurts, your indiscretions, and allowing the energy to move through you. Right after that thought came into my mind, the priest said the very same thing to the student! Simply put,

CHAPTER 12 | MEANING MATTERS, GOT MEANING?

confession is an opportunity to voice your doubts, fears, and flaws, hopefully without judgment, to bring them into the light of day. To see them for what they really are. Then you ask the big questions: What are my fears and doubts trying to tell me? What do I need to know? Followed by gratitude; telling your fears and doubts things like: I know you are just protecting me, I'm grateful for your care, Let's walk through this together and get to the other side.

When I was a little girl, about nine or ten years old, it was Christmas time, and our family had always done a gift exchange with some extended family members. Several weeks before the party, we drew names. My aunt got my name, and my mom asked me for gift ideas. There was only one thing I wanted. The new Donny Osmond album. I was so excited that I would be getting this new album and could hardly wait to open my present. When the time came to exchange gifts, I received mine, and it was a small box. I was heartbroken. I knew it wasn't my Donny Osmond album.

I kept my emotions in check, like I had been conditioned to do, while I opened the gift and found a beautiful watch. I smiled and thanked my aunt and immediately went to my room. When I got there, I closed the door and burst into tears. I was so depressed that I didn't get what I had asked for. My mom followed me into the room and asked what was wrong. When I told her, she got mad and said I was being ungrateful. I don't remember if I said this to her, I probably didn't, but in my mind, I was thinking these thoughts over and over: no one ever listens to what I say, what I say is not important, what I say doesn't matter.

Fast forward many years later, I am in my early 40's. I attended a workshop in Tacoma, Washington, and one of the exercises was to look at something that happened to us as a child that was not the outcome we had hoped for. We were instructed to write down the meaning we gave to the experience. We were then asked to choose two other meanings that experience could have had instead of the one that we assigned to it. Thinking about the Donny Osmond album experience, I had assigned the meaning that my voice didn't matter. As I thought about this, it was extremely hard to come up with two other meanings, as the hurt and pain were still so strong. We were told to step to the left of the experience and objectively find an alternative meaning, and then step to the right of the experience and objectively find a second alternative meaning. What I came up with was first, maybe my mom forgot to tell my aunt what I wanted, and second, perhaps my aunt felt that a watch would be a much more practical gift to have and enjoy for many more years than the latest trend in music. The purpose of the exercise was to look at the experience from a different perspective in order to try and tame the feelings we had attached to it. When I looked at it from these two perspectives, I was able to see that perhaps either one of them could also be true. And the amazing realization was that if either one of these two were the real truth, it had nothing to do with *who I was*! It was such a wonderful revelation of how powerful meaning can be, especially when it's of a negative nature. All these years, I have carried that judgment within me, that my voice doesn't matter, it's a waste of time to speak up, and it doesn't do any good to ask for what I want.

CHAPTER 12 | MEANING MATTERS, GOT MEANING?

A few months later, when my mom was visiting, I shared the story with her. I spoke about it in a light and loving manner. She listened, didn't say anything, and seemed to be thoughtful about it. Several months later, it was Christmas time, and my mom came to Washington state from Colorado to spend the holidays with us. When it was time to open our gifts, mom handed me one that was shaped like an album. It was the Donny Osmond album that I had asked for when I was a child! Mind you, this was many years after albums had gone out of style. In the previous decades, we had sailed through eight-track tapes, cassette tapes, and now CD's were the norm. I didn't even have a record player anymore, but I was so excited to get this album! I still have a few albums left in my collection. Most of the albums are by The Beatles, Paul McCartney, George Harrison, and John Lennon. I lovingly added Donny Osmond to my prized collection of albums. And still no record player! Maybe I'll ask for one for Christmas!

This is a great example of how we assign meanings to experiences that are detrimental to our emotional well-being. Of course, that wasn't the only experience that cemented the belief that my voice didn't matter. It was just one of many examples that proved to me in my formative years that this meaning was true for me. Now, as an adult, I have carried that baggage for years and years and years, and it's really hard to let go of that meaning. I've worked hard in the last few years to change it, and I have made great strides. Occasionally, however, an experience will happen, or a past situation will resurface, where my resolve is tested. Do I really believe that my voice matters? There's always that little child that felt offended, that felt belittled and invisible, and it tends to be the first reaction when I experience a situation where I don't feel like I'm being heard. It's that first unconscious reaction to shrink back and just be quiet. The difference is that I've become aware of it now, where in the past, I would immediately shrink back without knowing and just be that way. Now that I'm consciously making an effort to change it, I'm more easily aware of what's happening, which allows me to make the shift to the different meaning that my voice does matter. Then I can take action to speak my truth in a kind and loving way.

As I was recording the audiobook for my recently released solo book, *Great Loss, Greater Love: The Art & Heart of Navigating Grief*, I found four typos in the manuscript! Initially, I was so frustrated because, in the process of getting the book ready for publication, I hired an editor who reviewed it several times. It felt like I reviewed it 1,000 times, and of course, my publisher edited it as well. So, I was perplexed as to how we missed these typos.

But as I got to thinking further about it, I realized that I was reading the book from a totally different perspective than that of a writer or an editor. I was reading the book as a storyteller. My audiobook producer told me to read the story with emotion as if I was feeling it again so that I could convey my emotional state as I was reading it. There were even a couple times where I quoted music lyrics, and I sang them, which was an amazing thing for someone who has always been afraid to express their voice. I did also include a spoken version, in case the publisher feels that it's too terrible to include my singing!

CHAPTER 12 | MEANING MATTERS, GOT MEANING?

My point being is that reading the book from a storyteller standpoint put me in a totally different perspective where I could see, feel, hear, and understand what I was reading in a different way. And in that way, in that perspective, is where I found the errors. And they weren't anything major. Just words that weren't spelled wrong, but spelled in a different, yet still correct way. So spell check didn't catch them. And someone reading it other than myself, like my editor or publisher, for example, wouldn't necessarily have caught it either because the word was correct, it was just the wrong word, yet it still made sense in the sentence.

This is a perfect metaphor for what beliefs do for us, when we shift perspective even by physically stepping aside and placing our body in a different place, when we are thinking about those beliefs. When we step into a different place, a different perspective, that is when the door opens to see from another viewpoint. It helps and supports us to see it from a bigger picture standpoint, and usually, we are in a higher evolved state of mind than when we originally took on that belief. A fresh perspective, without the emotional attachment or drama, allows us to see it from an objective point of view. And that's where we can change it. That's where we can look at it, look at the other potential meanings that could have been assigned to it, and then make a conscious decision, a conscious choice, about what our new belief will be. Then we embody that new belief by assigning new emotional states to it. We provide our body with its new navigational coordinates to get us to that new belief while repetitively expressing and modeling our new ideal. This is how we get that belief successfully embedded into our life. It's like planting a seed. The new seed is the new belief that we plant into our inner soil. We give it all the nutrients, fertilizer, water, and sun, which is our own love, energy, and presence, that will allow it to root deep and grow strong and tall.

And that's how we elevate our lives. It's not just pretending to elevate emotions or to elevate our vibration. It's actually taking mental, spiritual, emotional, and physical action combined together in a truly meaningful way that begins to create and cultivate our new way of being.

Got meaning? Is it the highest meaning for you?

Go get the *highest meaning!* You deserve it!

Chapter Thirteen

The Wisdom Within
By Maggie Morris

Maggie Morris

Maggie is an Authentic Caring, Sensitive Soul with a Passion for nurturing others with her Soul love. Maggie lives her gifts of service to humanity through her generosity and her ability to ignite the flame in others to see their limitless possibilities. Maggie uses her intuition and connection with spirit to be an example of strength and courage to all she meets. Now, as an Author, Public Speaker, Life Coach, Mindfulness Master/Mentor, Meditation Facilitator, and Death Doula, Maggie continues to pursue her passions as well as help those she connects with to find healing. Maggie loves and lives to encourage others to passionately become their Authentic Self by choosing healing through letting go of limiting beliefs that hold you back. Namaste. You can reach Maggie through her website at www.whispersofwisdom.ca or through Facebook.

The Wisdom Within
By Maggie Morris

As soon as I signed up to write this chapter on wisdom, my "monkey mind" began to work on me with questions such as this:

What a daunting task this is?

What wisdom do you possess that others would possibly need or want?

Don't you think this is a book for scholars?

Oh my, you have really done it this time. Who are you kidding?

Silly girl, don't even try!

So I avoided it, walked away from it, gave into those seeds that my monkey mind had planted within me. That is, until today!

Something began to rise up in my soul. Something deep within began to bubble up to the surface as a volcano erupting deep down in the belly of my soul. As I stood in the kitchen with my hands in the sink, my soul began to rise up from the ashes of that fire in my spirit. I could feel it flooding in as my spirit began to respond to the doubt I had begun to believe since agreeing to write this chapter.

Enduring wisdom, for me, is about enduring and gaining wisdom in everyday life struggles. The big storms that flood in trying to take us down, as well as the little voices

CHAPTER 13 | THE WISDOM WITHIN

of negativity that try to rob us of living up to our full potential.

My spirit reminded me that:

You, Maggie, empower women on a daily basis to step into the power of who they truly are.

You, Maggie, empower women that they are enough!

You, Maggie, speak about the power of one, how one person can be the change in our world.

You, Maggie, have the ability to inspire hope in others and be the strength they need to see that potential within themselves.

You, Maggie, although afraid, will climb that muddy mountain just to learn the lesson in it.

So write about that! Write about how you learned to listen to the voice of wisdom from within.

Step up, get up and write from the wisdom within!

Those were the empowering words of encouragement that came from my own spirit. Words that gave me the courage to sit down and start writing this chapter on wisdom.

To write about wisdom, I first looked up a few meanings of the word. Webster's Dictionary defines wisdom as "*knowledge* and the capacity to make due use of it." Wikipedia further describes wisdom as the ability to think and act using knowledge, experience, understanding, common sense and insight. Wisdom is associated with attributes such as unbiased judgment, compassion, experiential self-knowledge and virtues such as ethics and benevolence.

I was taught by my Mindfulness Mentor that *knowledge comes from learning where wisdom comes from living.* There is so much to gain from that statement.

Although both of these definitions describe wisdom as knowledge learned, I also believe that all of us are born with intuitive wisdom.

From the moment we are born, most of us know how to breathe. We know instinctively to cry for food or comfort. We, *from birth,* have that intuitive wisdom! As we grow, our curiosity has us instinctively craving wisdom, yet as we seek that wisdom, we tend to look to outside sources to feed that craving. In my adult years, I decided to choose a different approach. I decided to seek that wisdom from within. And surprisingly, I found that source of wisdom could be found within. I also believe that quite possibly, the wisdom within teaches us a wisdom of greater value than the wisdom we seek through education.

You may be wondering how you can find that source within. Let me tell you that there are unlimited ways, each just as unique as the individual doing the seeking. I can share a few things that I did while seeking within. You will find your own sources as you journey within yourself to seek your soul wisdom.

For me, it began by learning to quiet and still my mind. For many years of life, and in my life circumstances, I had given my monkey mind free rein over my thoughts. I

CHAPTER 13 | THE WISDOM WITHIN

learned through the wisdom of mindfulness and meditation that I could reboot and reprogram that "Maggie monkey mind." I learned how to and began the reprogramming of my whole way of being. Now when my monkey mind comes to visit, I simply ask, what does it need from me? That is, because monkey mind is an emotional response or reaction directly related to my own state of mind. I went from feeling like a victim of my circumstances to learning the art of gaining wisdom and manifesting joy and growth within those circumstances. In both good or bad events of life, we can always gain knowledge and wisdom when we take time to pause, connect and be mindful. That is where we find our power, and own it!

I learned a long time ago that often, *miracles come wrapped in shit*. Yep, you read that correctly. Not a misprint, not a mistake but the absolute truth. And you, my friend, are the one who must do the work cleaning and polishing that miracle. Sometimes in this life we need to "wash things off" to see their true value. Not everything starts out as a masterpiece, most beautiful works of art take time and great effort to create.

To quote Rumi, "If you are irritated by every rub, how will you be polished?" You are the miracle, and you need to do the polishing to find your wisdom. We often think that trials come into our lives to knock us down and destroy us when they actually come to refine, polish and teach us wisdom.

I have learned through the years to look within at times of difficulty, to look through the eyes of my soul and see how a particularly nasty dirty circumstance can grow and refine me while teaching me wisdom. Wisdom doesn't always come to me as I am in the muddiness of that circumstance but often as I sit with it or reflect upon it I find the growth in it. If you find yourself sitting in a muddy situation right now in your life, allow yourself some time to rest, wash off and then get up and seek the wisdom from it.

Another way that I found wisdom is through gratitude. Living a life of gratitude changes your perspective on every situation you find yourself in. When my first thought of the day is one of gratitude, it changes the way I respond to most circumstances in that day. By beginning my day with gratitude, I am creating the atmosphere in which I choose to live.

A few years ago, I participated in a 30-day Gratitude Challenge. During that challenge, we were asked to journal every day on gratitude. I noticed during that challenge that my attitude began to change. There was a shift in my mindset. That simple challenge changed my way of life. I now try to make it an everyday practice to start my day with gratitude, and I truly believe that it has changed my mindset. Today, I encourage you to try a 30-day Gratitude Challenge and see the positive impact it can have on your life. Be bold and courageous, make decisions that will benefit your own personal growth. Seek wisdom through gratitude!

Another way that I found wisdom was to connect with my spirit source. Notice that I did not say my religious source. I personally believe the two are very different. To me, religion is a man-made practice where spirituality is a personal connectedness. I refer to my spirit source as God

CHAPTER 13 | THE WISDOM WITHIN

or spirit. You may refer to that source as something completely different. The Hebrew word "chokma" stands for wisdom both divine and human. So, connect with your "Chokma," for when you do, you will find wisdom. You can find the divine in religious settings, through yoga, meditation, in nature, in art and in ways as numerous as the depths of your imagination. Seek the divine in your soul, and you will find it. When you ask your creator, angels, guides and ancestors to show up in your life, they welcome the invitation and are ready to guide you in the journey of connecting with the divine. They may show up in prayers, dreams, visions, books, strangers, nature, through intuition, as well as other random (or are they really random?) occurrences. One thing I have found in life is that nothing happens by accident, and there is no such thing as coincidence. I believe that all things happen on purpose, for the purpose of wisdom, growth and healing.

Wisdom can also be found in solitude. Solitude is often seen as a lonely place, but I have found that solitude can often be a place of complete tranquility. A place to quietly reflect on the past or dream of the future or a place to just be in the now. In solitude, you can just be! Sometimes I just sit, close my eyes and be one with myself. No thoughts to process, no expectations, just be still. Being still is actually doing something! It is not the waste of time that we often tell ourselves that it is. Solitude serves to fuel our inner self. Choose to seek solitude and see it as a treasure and not as a punishment. As small children we have been sent to our rooms or "solitude" as a punishment, just imagine how wonderful it might have been if we had been sent there to seek wisdom instead. How different life could be if children were taught that solitude can be healing? In solitude, our souls can speak! In solitude, our inner self can heal, refresh and renew itself. In solitude, we can hear the wisdom of our higher self. That higher self within. That higher self that is not encumbered by limiting beliefs, self-doubt, ego or wounds this life has brought into our lives. The wisdom of our higher self is pure through the pure love of our creator. I encourage you to practice solitude, for in solitude, you may find your greatest wisdom.

Wisdom is also found in experience. Holy wow, the wisdom of experience could be a book all to itself and thicker than any book on the shelves if we took the time to write our wisdom of experiences. That wisdom found in experience usually cannot be found in a book because that wisdom must be lived. Oh, for sure, we try to pass on the wisdom of our experience to others, but I find that most humans need to learn that wisdom on their own. I have often struggled, as a mom, attempting to force my children to learn from my experiences, only to find that they cannot relate, as they don't yet see the value of my experiences because it may not be relevant to their lives at this time. I remember hearing in school that *experience is our greatest teacher,* but not fully understanding what that meant until later in my life. Yes, some things we can learn from the experience of others, but most things we do need to learn on our own. As parents we all teach our children not to touch a hot stove, but I promise you once they touch that hot burner, they quickly learn from that experience. If we look at our experiences as our greatest teacher, we can gain great wisdom from every one of those experiences in life. I invite you to choose to look at your life experiences as your

CHAPTER 13 | THE WISDOM WITHIN

wisdom teacher. You may see things differently if you look at circumstances as happening *for you* instead of to you.

Now in my sixties, I look at life through the looking glass of experience and the wisdom I have gained throughout those years. I invite you to slow down a little more. Life gets too hurried. We get so busy *doing life* that we forget to *live it.* Choose to live every moment! Enjoy the wonder of each new day, of each new experience. Set that inner child free again and allow yourself to be as curious as you were as a child. Be free! Remove the chains of expectations that limit your ability to live life to the fullest measure possible. Listen to music and sing along! Maybe even *dance!* Find and do those things that feed your soul! Don't get me wrong, I certainly understand that we all need to earn a living and be responsible for our families and our future but I encourage you not to lose yourself while doing it. Find the balance of responsibility and curiosity. Don't be afraid to try new things.

I sometimes wonder about the *what ifs of life.* What if I took more chances? What if I followed my soul's leading? What if, I followed my heart more? What if I threw away the agenda sometimes and just went for it? What if I took that new job for less money that was more aligned with my core values? What if I threw caution to the wind and traveled abroad for six months or went to stay at a monastery to deeply connect with myself? What if I wrote the books I wanted to write? What if I wrote more poetry or started that art project? Each of us has our own *what ifs of life.* I encourage you to take some time and look at life for a moment through the eyes of your "what ifs." I believe that true wisdom is in knowing what is truly important, as well as acknowledging those things that may no longer be important and letting them go. As you seek the wisdom within, be prepared to act upon what you may find, and like me, you may find a greater wisdom than you ever thought possible! You may even find yourself stepping out of your comfort zone and doing things you once thought impossible!

All the wisdom you need is already within you! Tap into the source within, and the power you need you will find because *you are the wisdom*, and *you are the power*! You carry with you the *wisdom* to heal your soul.

Stand Tall in Your Power

By Maggie Morris

Stand Tall

You are Love

Stand Tall

You are Compassion

Stand Tall in your Power

Do not let Life

Dim your Light

Do not let Strife

Dim your Light

CHAPTER 13 | THE WISDOM WITHIN

Stand Tall in your Power

Let Courage Rise
Let Strength Rise
Let Hope Rise
Let Inspiration Rise
Stand Tall in your Power

Let the Beauty of Love
Be your SuperPower
Stand Tall in The Power
Deep in your Soul
When you become Weary
Rest in that Power
When Stress comes In
Rest in that Power
When Fear Arises
Sit in that Power

The Power you Seek
Is Within You
The Wisdom you Seek
Is Within You

ENDURING WISDOM

The Love you Seek

Is Within You

Stand Tall in the Power

You are the Power

Chapter Fourteen

Turtle Wisdom
By Vanessa Plimley

Vanessa Plimley

Vanessa has a deep passion for life, and the desire to help others create and live one full of joy, gratitude and meaning. She is an enthusiastic life coach, author, and personal trainer.

Vanessa loves exploring her surroundings, fishing, surfing and is a happy soul on a holiday.

She splits her time between North America and Nicaragua. To read more of her adventures, or retain her services check out:

www.stokeyourfire.com,

stokeyourfire.wordpress.com,

vanessaplimley@gmail.com.

Turtle Wisdom
By Vanessa Plimley

What gifts will this day bring?

This is the first thought that bubbles up through my subconscious in the early dawn hour.

With eyes still closed, I smile, hearing the cacophony of birds singing outside our tent. Many of their calls I don't recognize, as we are in a new part of the country that we have not explored before.

The avian harmonies interweave the soft hoot of an owl, the gobbling of a wild turkey, and what sounds like a monster woodpecker excavating bugs out of the tree above. He is so incredibly loud that he sounds like he is chipping paint off our truck rather than digging into the bark.

I open my eyes to my dog having a pup dream in her bed and wonder what she sees in her mind as her feet run in the air, nose twitching to unknown dream smells. Rolling over, my husband's big blue eyes peek out from under the covers. His laugh lines convey a big hidden smile.

We are immediately giggling at the deflating bed, of how we froze in the night because the heater was turned to fan rather than heat. Of the massive thunderstorm lighting up the inside of our tent at midnight and the following torrent of rain adding to the grand performance. Of the dog

CHAPTER 14 | TURTLE WISDOM

cowering in the corner before crawling into the bed, trying to escape the wrath of the heavens.

The first gifts of this day are simple ones. Of hearing, love, warmth, and laughter.

It has become a ritual of mine to begin mornings with this question of curiosity, but also of deep gratitude for the small things that show up.

Emerging from the tent, it is the morning light glistening on a spider's dewy web that catches my eye. A deer gazing at me as she quietly munches fresh grass. A cup of tea to warm cool hands as the light comes up and the sun on my face as it burns off the mist, unveiling a glassy lake.

We are on time off in between work contracts and have embarked on a boating and camping trip through the South-Eastern USA.

As Canadians, it is fascinating how each state is so unique, with its change of accents, culture, flora, and fauna. We are so fortunate to have the time and means to explore such a vast and diverse country.

Yesterday was a logistics and workday, the inevitable tasks that need to happen when living life on the road. Managing businesses from afar and general online chores of paying bills, transferring money, and chasing down tax receipts. It is a time when technology is a blessing, to be able to sit at a campfire, pecking away at our laptops in a beautiful outdoor setting.

With this new day ahead, I decide to go down to the water and attempt to catch a fish.

With pure excitement, I organize rods and lures. The worn fishing box my father gave me overflows with a messy tangle of line and bobbers rescued from trees or found on the ground. I make a mental note to add its cleaning to the eventual to-do list and shove it into the backpack. With rods in one hand, I happily bike through the campground feeling like a ten-year-old heading out on a grand adventure.

Midweek in spring, the campground is empty, leaving a quiet beach to enjoy alone. My sudden arrival accidentally scares a snake into the water. He glides silkily along the shoreline, his head above and body beneath, leaving gentle ripples radiating out on the surface.

A blue heron silently glides overhead; the majestic grey body and widespread wings make me smile and think of my mother, as it is one of her favorite birds.

I cast a bobber and bait out into the depths and wonder what other creatures lie below. A wide smile of joy spreads across my face as the answer looks at me from beside a floating log. I see a beautiful turtle peering at me curiously. Along with her brightly colored head and mottled shell, I can see her clawed feet paddling the clear water, tail dangling in an adorable stubby point.

She ducks below the surface to emerge a few feet in front of me, then disappears once more to emerge in a new spot. She seems to be playing a cheeky game of peekaboo.

I brood about her eating my bait and pull it in rapidly to cast out further.

CHAPTER 14 | TURTLE WISDOM

It is always the same scenario when I attempt fishing in a new spot. I am so full of hope and complete ignorant surety that I will catch fish. Unfortunately, the results are a little more far between.

There is so much to learn depending on what kind of fish you want to catch, different bodies of water, change of depth, and bottom. Of salt or freshwater, and countries where fishing methods and varieties of fish found are completely different.

After a short time without success, I pull in my line, change my set up, and cast out again with renewed anticipation, the turtle quietly watching me. As time passes without a nibble, I realize I am probably rushing things and settle into a quiet pondering on a rock.

How content I am in nature. It's times like these I feel a part of my environment rather than just a visitor.

I worked many years as a hiking guide in the Canadian Rockies, spending summers outside, sharing the beauty of the wilderness with clients. After seasons of walking through the mountains, I began to sense a deep rhythm of the woods and its animals. The incredible system of life in balance from the smallest of bugs to the largest of beasts.

What an honor to witness such creatures in a protected habitat. The magnificent grizzly bear gorging on buffalo berries. Her massive head sweeping side to side, stripping entire branches of leaves and fruit. Her cubs nearby, romping and tussling in a fuzzy pile.

One season I was stunned to see a lone wolf padding down a deserted back road in the early dawn hour. His piercing yellow eyes resting on me as he passed by, his lanky steady gait taking him on a hidden mission to an unknown destination.

I would visit an osprey nest full of chicks, their fluffy heads protruding just above the woven rim.

Or crest an alpine meadow to see a lone mountain goat high on a barren slope, towering peaks and glacier behind, creating a breathtaking vision.

It would still be the height of summer, and I could sense the land preparing for Fall. Subtle hints like fading summer blooms and grasses subtly changing shade. Squirrels nibbling on mushrooms and transporting them away for their winter cache. Different smells in the air would accent cooler mornings.

In what seemed only weeks, the rapid transformation of the land was in all its glory. Reverberating bugles of elk in rut, creating a fall soundtrack to the symphony of color that would paint the mountainsides shades of gold, persimmon, and saffron.

I have always loved to be outdoors, my head to the sky and feet in the dirt. The dirtier my feet, the more fun I'm having.

I would spend hours in the woods as a kid. Attempting to make bow and arrow, mixing secret salves of my imagination from berries and mashed up leaves. Building forts to play in and spending hours under the protective branches of wise old trees. I felt more comfortable and safe there than anywhere else.

CHAPTER 14 | TURTLE WISDOM

I am a Heinz 57 breed of human. I thought a blend of English and Scottish, yet on a quiet afternoon stroll with my grandmother, she wove more colored threads into the tapestry of my family tree.

Quietly speaking, as her knotted hands gripped her walker, she told me that on one side of the family, my great-great-grandfather was Irish, and his wife was Native American Indian from the Plains Ojibwe or Saulteaux.

I could not find much information on their story, yet the knowledge struck a chord deep within me, like a different vibration of self. Perhaps it was confirmation of the connection I have always felt with the earth.

Growing up on the West Coast of Canada, I sought the deep woods, mountaintops, and the ocean for wisdom and answers.

With all my life challenges or difficult moments, I would escape to the wilderness. With desperate eyes streaming, I would wail to the wind or swim below the surface of the sea for the clicking reassurance of the creatures below.

This would not change with miles and time.

During many years of travel, I found myself on a far off shore running beside a growling storm out at sea. The wind rushing around and through me, adding to the turbulent questions of my purpose and life direction.

Or wandering through ancient woods in the fading afternoon light, fire gilding the edges of the leafy canopy above, and the wonderful feeling of spongy moss below my toes like a fragrant carpet. It reminded me to tread lightly on this fragile earth and respect and love her creatures.

Crossing oceans by sailboat, sitting under a full moon, its light dancing on the sea, filled me with such a deep connection to God or a higher power. The buzzing energy of life crackling over all the cells in my body, leaving such a sweet agony gripping my heart.

With nature, I can breathe deeply and remind myself of my inner wisdom without all the chatter or opinions of others. I can ask questions and navigate with my inner compass.

It reminds me to live deeply in the current moment. Not in the past or the unknown road ahead. To not dream away days or weeks or months, even when in a challenging chapter of life.

During this trip, I reached out to some people in my life to ask what wisdom meant to them. The answers were as vast as the variety of people themselves.

For some, it is external study, the gathering of information, applying it and sharing it with the world. For others, it is to be open to the inevitable changes life brings. Or allowing views to change over time with additional information gathered.

Wisdom for some people is a culmination of personal lessons learned, to be shared and passed down through generations, culture, or society. For others, it's the spiritual journey one discovers or lives during a lifetime.

A wonderful friend wrote, "Wisdom is enjoying life!" Amen to that.

I have deep respect for people who dedicate their lives to study. Whatever their focus, their search for and addition of knowledge for humankind is impressive. I have respect for

CHAPTER 14 | TURTLE WISDOM

those that pledge their life to God or a spiritual existence. Of people who choose to devote their time to raising a family.

At middle age, I realize, the more I know, the less I know, I know. We all walk such unique paths in our own personal universe, with an individual calling, purpose, reality, and perspective. How boundless is the human experience, how varied are the ways we traverse this earth, and the lessons we gather along the way.

When I reflect on my own idea of wisdom, it is living deeply and enjoying a full life. Of learning, celebration, and connection. Of a life filled with love and adventure.

Of living my purpose; to share joy and inspire others to find theirs.

Wisdom to me is appreciating and honoring others' individuality. Of loving and respecting myself with all the light and dark, with the intention to grow and change like the tide washes a beach, shifting sand and rocks leaving it new each day.

To have the courage to keep an open heart and mind so that I might recognize the beautiful people who enter my life, to teach me, and help me grow. To listen and learn.

Or the wisdom of being present enough to savor a morning on a lake, with a turtle.

I look for her and she has pulled herself up onto a log to sun herself. I realized a few days ago that I have seen turtles almost every day of our trip. Paddling across the secluded cove where we have anchored our boat, sitting in the grass in our campsite, or crossing the roads after a night of rain.

My husband and I had a book about spirit animals or totems. Often we would look up the meaning or significance when a creature kept showing up in our lives.

It seems every year I have had a different animal that would continually appear in dreams, in books, in art or conversation. I adopt them as my theme, their meaning or symbolism always a direct correlation of what I am learning or experiencing at the time.

My last few years have been of orca, owl, and fox. This year it seems that turtle is swimming into my life.

Turtle wisdom or significance is different for each culture, in history or spirituality. For some Native American tribes, it represents the connection to mother earth and the creation of North America called Turtle Island. When I looked up "Turtle Wisdom" online, the first few lines I read were so fitting. They read, when the turtle shows up in your life, it is to remind you to slow down and investigate the wonder around you. To stay true to your path and be at peace with your choices.

I smile and think of how we are like a turtle these days, traveling with our home on our back. Of feeling content where we are in this moment. Having time to go inward and take stock or reflect. Of how our lives are moving at a slower pace, so we can enjoy all the gifts that show up in our day.

CHAPTER 14 | TURTLE WISDOM

Turtle reminds me, that with a slower pace, we can observe the world more closely. Not only does she remind me of this in nature but in people.

So often we are rushing, emerged in our own busy lives, we lose touch with those around us. By slowing down, connecting and listening to others, we can witness the small changes or shifts within them and read between the lines for unspoken longing or desire.

We can have a conversation with a stranger to find out their wonderful life story. You never know who you will meet or what wisdom they hide beneath the exterior shell they let the world see.

Turtle wisdom may be for this year, but the lessons gathered, I will carry with me into the future unknown. For today, this turtle reminder is such an expansive gift. What else will this day bring I can't imagine.

I am jerked out of my philosophizing on the shoreline when I feel my rod bounce.

The line begins to spool out, setting my reel buzzing. I am surprised to feel there is a good-sized fish on the end. I am squealing with delight as I reel it in, and discover a big ol' catfish with its thick dripping whiskers and bulbous eyes.

I keep him in the water as I gently pull out the crimped hook. After telling him how beautiful he is and apologizing for the mouth puncture, I quickly set him free back to the deep where he disappears with such speed, his perfect coloring hiding him from above.

I am rather proud of myself and grinning stupidly on the shore.

ENDURING WISDOM

With eyes shining, I look at the turtle. "Did you see that?"

I am almost hugging myself, I am so happy. Gazing around, I nod my head.

The line in a song by Ray Wylie Hubbard comes to me:

"And the days that I keep my gratitude higher than my expectations, well I have really good days."

Chapter Fifteen

Don't Be a Knock Off, the Original is Always Better
By Samantha Renz

Samantha Renz

Samantha Renz is the CEO of Evolving Texas and the Founder of The Soul Tea Foundation. She has over 22 years of experience in civil engineering and planning. Samantha, a high school dropout, was able to find a second chance at life because someone who held the belief that more was possible encouraged and mentored her. She holds the belief that you are not defined by your past and has a vision to create second chance opportunities, which backs The Soul Tea Foundation Mission of empowering individuals with mentorship and training through Soul Tea's Success Path. Samantha is also the President and Chief Love Officer at Soul Tea, PBC, a mission-focused franchise Tea Shop that offers jobs and mentorship to opportunity-challenged individuals.

Samantha received her Civil Engineering Degree at the University of Texas at Arlington in 2009. She is licensed in seven states, and under her direction, the Evolving Team has completed hundreds of land development and municipal infrastructure projects.

As CEO of Evolving Texas, Samantha assumes the integral role of developing and leading strategic growth, as well as nurturing client partnerships. Additionally, she works tirelessly to create the outstanding workplace culture enjoyed by the Evolving Team. As part of this culture, Samantha has implemented the Evolving Cares program, which has resulted in Evolving employees tutoring the A&E Drafting class at Texans CAN Academy, supporting the STEM program and helping kids who have struggled in a traditional high school environment.

In her spare time, Samantha enjoys volunteering, traveling, attending art and music events and spending time with her friends and family. Her personal mission statement is "I will make the world around me better one intentional action at a time."

Don't Be a Knock Off, the Original is Always Better
By Samantha Renz

Do you know who you are? Do you live every day as your true self? I would say that most of us in this world do not, and those who do are on a path to enlightenment. I do not know if we can ever truly reach a state of enlightenment in this life, where we live in that place 100% of the time, but if others have reached it, I applaud them. It is not easy. It is not easy to let go of and walk away from the beliefs in our head, the emotions, or the ego. It is not easy to question everything we have been taught and to learn to do differently. It can be torturous and confusing to question the core values and things you have believed to be true your entire life.

I have often heard it said that integrity is doing the right thing even when no one is watching. What about authenticity, and what is the right thing? Is the right thing the ideas taught by our parents? The brainwashing from different religious institutions? Societal norms? Things that are considered "acceptable" in the different situations throughout our lives?

This was the start of the battle inside of me. Asking the question, "Do I believe this because it is true, or do I believe this because I was told or taught to believe it?" As a child, I believed my parents, I believed my teachers, I believed people older than me, I believed what I read in

CHAPTER 15 | DON'T BE A KNOCK OFF THE ORIGINAL IS ALWAYS BETTER

books, I believed the pastor at my church, the youth leaders, and anyone in authority. I was not taught in any way to question authority or my elders. My instinct was to question, but I ignored my instinct and suffered because of it.

Because of the unquestioned beliefs, I was sexually abused and believed my abuser's threats, I held on to religious baggage and lived in constant fear of not being good enough to make it to heaven, I believed I could never be accepted for who I am because I am a homosexual. I believed that I was not acceptable or loveable for who I am. That manifested in me as a need to earn love and acceptance, hide my true self and show the world what I thought they thought would be acceptable and make me loveable.

I want to state a quote here because it resonates with me. Georgia O'Keefe said, "I have already settled it for myself, so flattery and criticism go down the same drain, and I am free."

As I sit here writing this, I struggle with judgment. I am not a professional writer by any means. I have read and erased, backspaced, and questioned the lines I had written. I paused for a moment and said a prayer, and asked for my true authentic self to be present and write this. I would like my ego to stand down and fear of what any reader may think to be removed from my thoughts as I write. Authenticity is my goal.

What I have found, though, is that curiosity along with authenticity is the key. When I look at people in my life that have claimed to be believers in Christ and followers of

God's word, what they feel is authenticity is speaking what they believe to be true. Doing what they believe to be right. The incongruence I feel here is that where that individual resides in this life and in this world is sometimes (not always) in a place where they have put their stake in the ground and claimed a belief or something they were told or taught. My question to each of them and to each of you is, "Have you gotten curious enough to question your own beliefs?" If not, why not? That would be my challenge in this chapter. Question what you believe and why, ask questions of yourself and others, and get to know you.

When I asked the questions, I found that most of my foundational beliefs were based on what I was taught and what I thought was right and wrong based on the religious teachings I had encountered in my life and based on my family and societal norms. I believed in a judgmental God that was waiting to send people to hell. I believed there was a checklist I needed to fulfill even though I knew that Jesus had died on the cross for me. I not only had to believe, accept it, and repent (or turn away) from my sin. I had to choose a different path for that blood and forgiveness to be there for me. Not just for me, though, others too. How can you be raised in such a manner and not grow into an adult that is without a form of judgment? Is it judgment to say, "The Bible says if you do not believe in Jesus as your savior, you will burn in hell"? For me, it felt like I was living in a place of judgment. I was also living in a place of fear for other souls. Also, I was living in a place of compassion for every one of those souls. I looked up the definition of judgment in *Webster's Dictionary,* and one of the definitions was "an opinion or decision that is based on

CHAPTER 15 | DON'T BE A KNOCK OFF THE ORIGINAL IS ALWAYS BETTER

careful thought" another definition is "the act or process of forming an opinion or making a decision after careful thought." How often do we do this? I have formed opinions of others and would not have considered it judgment, but authentically, that is what it is.

When we talk about God, it is often a biblical version of God, and that is the God I was taught to believe in. Even that Bible defines God as love. 1 John 4:16 says, "God is Love." This has been a contradiction in my life because I was also taught that God is jealous. That same Bible says love is not jealous and does not get puffed up. I have gotten curious. One thing I realized is that my whole life, I tried to fit in "the box" I was supposed to fit in, and I never fit. Through all my questioning and curiosity, I realized that I had been trying to put God in a box, and He does not fit. He is who He is, and I am who I am. I am also connected to Him.

In my curiosity, I went outside of my normal thinking and even set out to prove myself wrong. I have read and researched so many things. I have landed in a place where I believe there is a God. That is what I call Him. Some call him creator, some call Him spirit, some call Him source, and others call Him by different names. I have been an adoptive parent, stepmother and friend to many children who have all called me by different names, and I know without a doubt when they call my name, whatever they call me, I know they are talking to me.

Now let us dive in. Do you ever find yourself playing different roles in your life? Are you one way with your family, and another with your friends? Are you one person at work and a different person at home? Do you know why you believe what you believe? Are you passing it on as truth? Do you speak authentically and say what you truly feel? Does being around people drain you? Sometimes that drain comes from keeping on our masks. Keeping the smile on our face. Putting up the brave front. Do you put up walls? Do people really know you? Do you know you? I was told as a young adult, "If you don't let people know who you really are, they cannot love the real you, and you will never truly feel loved." This was such a true statement. It rang true for me well into my adult life.

I would like you to ponder a question with me. Who are you? There was a time in my life when if I were asked the question, "Who are you?" that I would have answered, "I am Samantha Renz." I know now that I am not a collection of letters, and that is just the name that I was given. I am not my story. I am not a sum of the places I have lived and the things that I have done. I am not the result of bad relationships or good ones. I am not the sum of my mistakes. I am not defined by my past. Those are things that happened to my body here on Earth, and the pain was experienced by my pain body. That is not me.

I am an eternal being who has value and who has worth. I would say the same of you. You are an eternal being with worth and value. When you look in the mirror, what reflection do you see? Do you realize you are the most amazing creation on all the Earth? The body you see when you look in the mirror is a vessel for your beautiful spirit, and your mind and all of it together make up who you are. Have you been trying to fit into a box? I will tell you now, you will not fit in one if you are your authentic self. Only

CHAPTER 15 | DON'T BE A KNOCK OFF THE ORIGINAL IS ALWAYS BETTER

you can be you, and this world needs you. Love who you love, be who you are, speak your truth. That is how you change the world. You might want to be a seamstress, an artist, a poet, a writer, a teacher, a graphic designer, a storyteller, a historian, an insurance agent, a mobile stylist, a pet groomer, a janitor, a scientist, a doctor, a politician, a parent, a transcriptionist, or an individual like no other who no one can relate to, and that is exceptional!

Once again, I refer to *Webster's Dictionary*. It states that a knockoff is "a copy that sells for less than the original broadly; a copy or imitation of someone or something popular." Do not be a knockoff—be the original you. The only you.

You do not have to fit into a box to bring value to this world. In fact, you bring more value when you do not fit in a box. How does the world benefit from duplicates? Knockoffs are of less quality, they are cheaper, and they are sold on street corners. The original has value. Do not be a knockoff. Be you!

This brings me to my original point of authenticity and the question I asked. Who are you?

Let us talk about who you are. I would love it if you would take a break from reading, pull out some paper, and write about who you are. As stated in the opening paragraphs, I believe that who you are is worthy and valuable. I also believe that who you are is separate from your ego and who you try to be. Who you are is your authentic self.

Living authentically is powerful and freeing. At its core, authenticity is about being your true self. To be your true self, one needs to be self-aware. Self-awareness is the first step in taking control of your life. Where you choose to focus your thoughts, emotions, and reactions will determine where you will end up in life. From the moment we are born, we start moving away from our true selves. As we go through life, we are molded by our parents, society, etc. We begin to depend on our egos as a false sense of protection. We build walls and naturally want to stay within our comfort zones. Staying in our comfort zones keeps us limited and from exploring our true selves, our own wants and needs and from having real, authentic relationships with others and ourselves.

If you want to explore being your true self and becoming self-aware, the first step is to start listening to yourself, your inner thoughts and your body. Our body has a way of letting us know what we need. When you feel anxious and uncomfortable or have a knot in your gut, when you feel tense in a situation, these are all signs that your body is trying to get you to pay attention. Something is wrong. Normally what is wrong is that you are being asked or feel like you should do something that feels inauthentic to you. Meaning it does not align with your values.

Speaking of values, that is the next step. You may want to define some values for yourself. To do this, it is often helpful to answer the question, "What do I want?" What do you want for your life? For example, I want peace. For me, peace is the absence of anxiety; it is quiet stillness in my body, an absence of frustration, and knowing I am being true to myself.

Values can be anything you choose. They are a guideline for how you will live your life and what you want in your

CHAPTER 15 | DON'T BE A KNOCK OFF THE ORIGINAL IS ALWAYS BETTER

life. I value love. That means loving myself first. It means responding to others in a loving way. It means tough love at times. It means setting and holding my boundaries. It means respecting the boundaries of others. It means allowing myself to be who I am. It means allowing others to be who they are.

Self-awareness is necessary if you want a strong character. You want to trust yourself and others and be trustworthy. It is also how we maintain openness, authenticity, and vulnerability. Self-awareness is paying attention to our thoughts and behavior and becoming curious about our emotions and reactions. It means understanding our own moods, desires, and feelings. Instead of judging ourselves or trying to avoid these things, we observe them, acknowledge them, and let them flow through us when necessary.

Accepting your self is also a large part of authenticity and self-awareness. Many times, we tend to think when we do not fit in a particular box that we are not good enough. You are perfectly and wonderfully made. You were not made to be anyone but you. Learn to accept and love yourself for who you are and if there is something that does not align with your values, change that. Do not worry about changing the things that are originally you.

To recap, to become more authentic, we need to become more self-aware. A few steps we discussed are: 1) knowing what we want, 2) listening to ourselves, 3) identifying our values, 4) acceptance of who we are. In addition to these items, truth-telling is important. That is being honest with your self and others.

In addition, learn to recognize and own your strengths and weakness. If we know these things and are authentic with others about them, it leads to real vulnerable conversations and relationships.

Being self-aware and authentic leads to being your true self. I love don Miguel Ruiz's four agreements found in his book *The Four Agreements*. These are: 1) become impeccable with your word, 2) do not take anything personally, 3) don't make assumptions, and 4) always do your best. If you can remember these four things and do your best to live by them, it will be a huge step towards authenticity and acceptance of yourself.

In the end, authenticity is the greatest gift we can give ourselves and to this world. All the great inventions, the great discoveries, were one of a kind. You are one of a kind; you are an original masterpiece. There is no other like you. Remember to stay genuine, and don't be a knockoff!

Chapter Sixteen

Is that Gucci Luggage You Are Carrying?
By Dr. Carra S. Sergeant

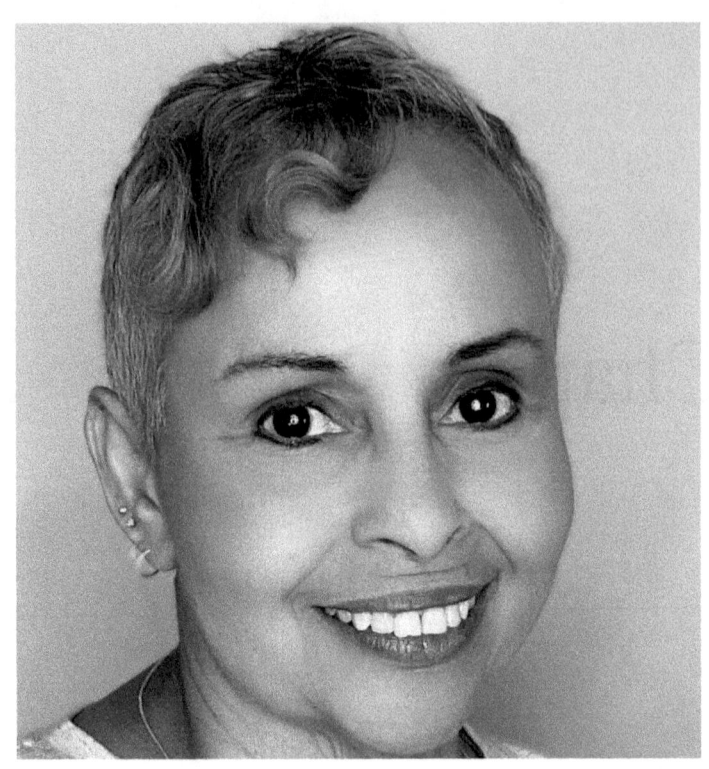

Dr. Carra S. Sergeant

Dr. Carra S. Sergeant is a Licensed Professional Counselor, a Certified Clinical Hypnotherapist, and an Access Bars Practitioner. She is the owner of Peace from Pieces Counseling Center, located in Lake Charles, Louisiana. Dr. Sergeant works with teens, adults and couples and is particularly passionate about facilitating healing from trauma and helping clients work through anxiety disorders. Details on all the services provided by Dr. Sergeant can be found on her website at: www.peacefrompieces.net.

Dr. Sergeant's alter-ego, Carra, is a "when life gives you lemons, add liquor and make a lemon cello" kind of woman. She is daring, caring, bold, and, at 65 years, some people may call her old. She lives in Louisiana with her life partner, 3 dogs, 2 parrots and 2 cats. She enjoys boxing, quilting, and reading.

Acknowledgments

They say it takes a village, and I am so grateful for mine:

- James and Susan Sergeant: Mom and Dad, I can still feel you here with me.
- Glenn Sergeant, my big brother and my rock: I have no words to express my deep love for you.
- Monica, Ashley and Glenn, Jr.; my nieces and nephew: thank you for loving me unconditionally.
- Sandra Castille, my twin soul: I love you for being my touchstone.
- Jerry and Kacey Noland: I am honored to be your M-2. Kassidy and Braden, you are my special gifts.
- MeMe McKerley, my bonus mom: you have been a blessing in my life. Love also to my many extended McKerley family members.
- Andrea Vidrine: I will *always* be grateful.
- K. Scott, my "Sissy": I thank the universe daily for you.
- Karen Woodard and Sarah Brink: I love you, my spirit sisters.

Last but *most* importantly, Nannelle Noland: For 25 years, you have been my brightest light, my biggest cheerleader, and my greatest love.

Is that Gucci Luggage You Are Carrying?
By Dr. Carra S. Sergeant

Before reading this chapter, I would like you to take three deep, cleansing breaths. Open your mind to the possibility of new revelations, new insights and new concepts. I'd like to see you set an intention that you will get exactly what you need *today* from reading this chapter. Set an additional intention that what you don't need today (or don't realize you need today) will plant in your unconscious mind, waiting to blossom into beautiful flowers of wisdom for you later on. Take three additional deep breaths to seat those intentions.

How do you define life? Merriam-Webster posits the definition to be: the quality that distinguishes a vital, functional being from a dead body; the sequence of physical and mental experiences that make up the existence of an individual. Some keywords jump out to me: vital, functional, sequence, mental, physical. These words collectively describe the components of a well-lived life. But one word stands out in that it indirectly seems to speak to the quality of that well-lived life: *experiences*. It implies that, at the bottom of it all, life is a collection of experiences that carry us from birth to death, and how we perceive or interpret those experiences determines the quality of our life.

CHAPTER 16 | IS THAT GUCCI LUGGAGE YOU ARE CARRYING?

All of my friends and family know that when the Harry Potter books were written, I immediately became a huge Harry Potter fan. At first, I was mesmerized by the exquisite writing style and vivid imagery that literally jumped off the pages. I noticed that kid in me loved Harry's magical, wide-eyed excitement as he stepped off that train into his destiny and grew to know so much about the mystical world in which he found his tribe.

Even at this age, I still am a die-hard Harry Potter fan. The reasons now, however, have significantly broadened. It isn't about the fantasy, the magic, or the smoke and mirrors. It's because the Harry Potter books give us a snapshot of how to:

Accept yourself - in spite of

Love others - in spite of

To be ok - in spite of

To survive - in spite of

And above all,

See life as a wondrous adventure, *in spite of*

In *Harry Potter*, all of the standard plot components of a best seller are there: Boy enters new school; makes friends and enemies; falls in (and out of) love; fights for what he feels is right; experiences the entire spectrum of emotions; grows into adulthood; marries, has family and (by implication), lives happily ever after. If, however, you allow yourself to step from behind the fantasmagorical curtain and consider the feelings you experience through the book's characters, the list is quite different and includes:

Excitement/apprehension

Comfort/fear

First love/first heartbreak

New friend/lost friends

Camaraderie/hostility

Death/rebirth (in a metaphorical sense)

If we take the whole library of Harry Potter books and look at them through those paired words, it, in addition to being a set of beautifully written books, we can also see that they collectively define life: The good, the bad, and the ugly. How awesome is it that a young boy understands this concept better than most of us adults? And Harry is clear on one thing: magic does not fix the pain of it all.

We have all felt pain, and, as a result, we all have baggage. The older we get, the more baggage we tend to carry. What, however, would you do if I, today, could give you some pointers on how to lighten that load? Would you want to? It would take a lot of work and practice, so would you seriously want to be able to step into and stand in your power?

CHAPTER 16 | IS THAT GUCCI LUGGAGE YOU ARE CARRYING?

Life is a mish-mash of events and experiences, and no one comes out unscathed, so close your eyes for a second and rumble quickly through the junk in your baggage. What is in there due to experiences you have had in your life? What is in there because you created it? Was any of it controllable? Just jump in and dig through. Why is it in there? Why did we put it in there?

So here is the mind-blowing revelation I promised: It is not the experience that creates the baggage; it is how we perceive and process the experience that creates the baggage.

Once again: It is not the experience that creates the baggage; it is how we perceive and process the experience that creates the baggage.

In a nutshell, *we* create all the baggage that we carry through life. The gift is that, at the foundation of that one line, is the message that we can, if we choose to, seek another way to process our experiences so that they just become part of our story, not part of our baggage. Please do not hear this as a criticism because it is not. We are human, and on any given day, we can only do the best that we can do on *that* day. Some days are better than others, yet, despite our best efforts, we are still left with some new stuff in our baggage.

Most of us live life in a state of duality:

Good vs. bad

Holy vs. evil

Black vs. white

ENDURING WISDOM

Smart vs. stupid

Rich vs. poor

And the list goes on and on. Sadly enough, in this state of duality, we pigeonhole our lives to one of the two far ends of the spectrum, and, in doing that, we do not allow ourselves to see or experience all beautiful rich shades in the middle. Guess what though, the "real" story is found at the center, and any needed "real" healing is generally found smack dab in the middle. I call the harmful end of that spectrum the "Let's add some crap to our baggage" cycle.

As humans, we assign "value points" to every experience we have, and those points generally fall under two categories: good or pain. What, however, if you could see things as neither good nor bad. Fantastic, fun, joyful are other words to substitute for "good." Sad, nasty, uncomfortable are acceptable words to substitute for bad. In other words, rather than label the experience, describe the experience. That way, you have a path to re-experience your happier memories and a framework within which you can process your less-than-happy ones.

Let's examine what the "baggage packing" phase looks like:

> Wow! Guess what happened to me?
>
> Oh my God, it hurt so much
>
> I can't believe that happened
>
> I can still feel the pain as if it were yesterday

CHAPTER 16 | IS THAT GUCCI LUGGAGE YOU ARE CARRYING?

> It happened so long ago; will the pain ever stop?
>
> The wound is still there. See?
>
> It's nasty, isn't it?

Memory experts say that if you hear something three times, it attaches to a neural pathway in our brain, so for the third time: It is not the experience that creates the baggage; it is how we perceive and process the experience that creates the baggage.

To make good use of this concept, you have to allow yourself to go through whatever pain you need to go through to heal. There is no "sweeping it under the rug," no "just forget about it," and no "just get over it." This process reminds me of a cheer we had in high school. So, become your own cheerleader and repeat after me: if you are somewhere that you can stand up and talk out loud, do so; if not, quietly, *but loudly* in your head, repeat each line after me:

We gotta tear that wall down

Okey dokey

We can't go over it

We can't slide under it

We can't go around it

We gotta go *through* it

Okey dokey

Let's just go!

While the cheer is about winning, we need to understand that winning is not always about vanquishing the enemy, which in most cases is pain. It is about putting the pain *in its place* within the context of our life. The only way to do that is to process the feelings. So let me say one important thing about feelings. For most people, anger is the "go-to" emotion. We feel safe behind a wall of anger. *Anger*, however, *is* generally *a secondary emotion*. It is the blockade we put up to keep the real feeling at bay. It makes us look strong and powerful. Anger is the emotion that we grab so we can avoid the truly uncomfortable feelings that sit right below the surface.

At some point in working through pain, we need to take a brief detour and consider the lessons that particular pain taught us. When we begin to consistently process pain through the filter of what did we learn, the *lessons* are what we start to carry—not that pain. Yes, the pain can and does sometimes just come and go as it pleases, but the trick is holding on to the lesson and releasing the pain. Let it flow through. Do not give it a home inside of your heart, your mind, or your body. That is not an easy task because, as you probably already know, your body keeps score. It holds all the hurt, the pain, the trauma you have ever experienced. If you try to run and hide from it, rather than processing it, the dis-ease it creates within your body turns into actual disease.

CHAPTER 16 | IS THAT GUCCI LUGGAGE YOU ARE CARRYING?

I have an acronym that I use as a handy tool to try to ease the blow of pain if I see it coming at me: F C C.

F - can I fix it

C - can I control it

C - can I change it

If the answer is no to all three of those questions, walk away gracefully, unless you are in danger, in which case — *run!*

A great example is when we feel a dearly loved friend pulling away; we torture ourselves with questions like: What did I do? What did I say? How can I fix it? We cry, whine, beg, plead, cajole and try to hang on as long as possible. In the end, the friendship is burnt to a crisp because of the drama we brought to it. The scenario could look something like this:

Someone you loved dearly was suddenly feeling distant. You ask what is wrong, and the response is "Nothing." "But you feel so distant." "I am not," is the reply. From their perspective, they are speaking their truth, but when in pain, our truth is all we care about. We continue to puzzle, and query and secretly cry because we know our friend is "leaving." But without some missing information, it is difficult to process that pain. There is a saying that "some people come into your life for a reason and some only for a season," but there are always lessons they leave with you.

To address the standstill, if we process the issue internally, utilizing the FCC framework:

F: Is there anything we can do to fix this?

Something beyond our reach is different, so *nope*!

C: Is there anything we can do to change it?

There is no solid concrete information to go on, so *nope*!

C: Is there anything we can do to control it?

We must not attempt to control human beings, so *nope*!

The only decision to be made here is to open your arms and let that friend go. By not dumping all your needy drama in their lap, the friendship has a chance to take a new form, and you would be able to still have that person in your life. New and strangely different, probably not as close, but still a friend.

If we were to decide today that we did not want to carry Gucci luggage anymore, the process might look like this:

> Girl, guess what happened to me?
>
> It happened awhile ago
>
> And it hurt like hell
>
> I remember it like it was yesterday

(Dear readers, here's where we *totally* flip the script.)

CHAPTER 16 | IS THAT GUCCI LUGGAGE YOU ARE CARRYING?

But I am thankful it doesn't hurt like it used to

Yes, it definitely left a scar, but I call it

My battle scar cuz it means I *survived*.

Be a warrior! Be a survivor! Filter your experiences through the kaleidoscope of all feelings that are afforded you. Your life will be richer and fuller if you can fully process your pain instead of squirreling it away in some expensive baggage.

I love life! I have lots of scars and lessons and, yes, even some baggage. Life is dirty and grimy yet joyful and loving. I embrace it and value *all of it*. When I reach my finish line, I do not want to be a dusty hull of a human. I want to come skidding over the home plate with bloody knees and bruised elbows and mud streaks on my face screaming at the top of my lungs: Wow, what a friggin' ride! Can I go again?

And *that*, dear readers, is my wish for you.

Chapter Seventeen

Say the Magic Words
By Lindy Chaffin Start

Lindy Chaffin Start

Entrepreneur coach and marketing maven Lindy Chaffin Start provides entrepreneurs with insight, strategy, and advice to help them identify their highest purpose and passion and achieve their business goals. She creates marketing strategy and creative as unique and authentic as their company that builds trust with their audience. You can reach Lindy through her website

www.unstoppablestart.com

or via email at lindychaffin@att.net.

Say the Magic Words
By Lindy Chaffin Start

How many times in your life have you desired beautiful words?

Think about it.

Romantic, loving, supportive words from your partner, words of encouragement from your parents, an "attagirl" from your sibling or best friend: words give life meaning. They, in their single- and multi-syllable way, can bring heartache, breathe life, and take away someone's magic in a whisper.

When I was a little girl, I wanted to be just like Olivia Newton-John. I was six years old when I received her *Totally Hot* album for my birthday. I must give it to my parents for being brave enough to give this to me along with the *Grease* soundtrack (I did say I wanted to be just like her) and Earth, Wind, and Fire's *Mirror Image* album. And as much as I loved singing along to *September*, and still do, the songs from *Totally Hot* made me want to sing, dance, and perform. Couch cushions turned up to make my baby girl stage; I would emerge as if from behind curtains to sing into a paper towel tube. My heart soared at the idea of one day becoming just like Olivia.

CHAPTER 17 | SAY THE MAGIC WORDS

IT ONLY TOOK ONE UGLY WORD

I continued to sing for many years, emotion always showing on my face, feeling the energy and passion that went into creating the songs I loved to sing. Then one day, sometime around third grade, the person I considered to be my best friend in the whole world told me I looked stupid when I sang. She told me I should keep a straight face and never show emotion. Her words cut deep. So deep I rarely sang again after hearing them. With those tiny, little, ugly words, she took away part of my magic.

I don't use the word magic lightly, though. When I was young, I discovered I had quite a bit of magic. I could see, hear, and feel things that most people could not. Some people liken these abilities to being psychic, but it was, is, just a sensitivity to spirit and energy, being empathetic or empathic. I was so confounded and intrigued by the things I experienced I started checking out every library book I could on witches, ghosts, the afterlife, anything considered occult back in 1980, which was anything paranormal that people didn't understand. I was eight.

My father was raised by a practical, stern Army dad and mom whose magic and passion were stolen from her causing her to commit suicide when my father was 10. My father could not understand my interest in the subject and told me he didn't want me reading those sorts of books. My mother being a good, supportive wife, agreed with him and wouldn't let me check them out from the library any longer, at least not while she was with me.

It didn't stop my many experiences, though and, as time passed, I began to see that my mother and my aunt were both quite sensitive themselves. They didn't acknowledge it; I can only assume because they would not have been supported either. Though still, they giggled over candles that would relight spontaneously and squeaks in floors when no one else was around.

When Father traveled and Mother and I were home alone, we might be visited by spirit. One time I recall I was introduced to a young girl who had been killed on the property where our home was built. She showed up for me as I was half awake, half asleep. She came into my room and looked at me, desperate for me to follow her, her eyes pleading. She turned and walked out the bedroom door, down the hall, where there was a loose floorboard that squeaked when you walked on it. I heard the floor moan under her steps and opened my eyes. Moments later, my mother came into my room, asking if I'd heard someone walking down the hall.

"Yes, I did."

She, as any strong woman would, investigated the house to make sure doors and windows were locked and no one else was present. When she returned to my room, she asked me who I thought was walking around the house. I told her about Amy, the little girl who had been murdered and how she had come into my room before walking down the hall. For the first time since telling me I shouldn't check out the

CHAPTER 17 | SAY THE MAGIC WORDS

occult books from the library, she acknowledged my sensitivity.

HERE WE GO AGAIN

I held onto my magic for a few more years until I was told I was stupid for thinking it was anything more than my mind playing tricks. There was that word again—stupid. I was told by someone I cared deeply for that what I believed, knew to be true, was not only incomprehensible but impossible. My heart was broken. My magic went away. The experiences disappeared. My mind, body, and spirit felt dead from those few tiny, ugly words.

Because I denied my gifts, what followed was long nights full of night terrors. I would awaken to snakes and spiders large enough to eat me, shadows of people standing in the corners of the room watching me. I would sit straight up in bed and watch them in the room with me, waiting for them to swallow me up. Watching as snakes slithered under the bed just below me, or spiders hovered inches above my face, left me paralyzed for fear they would drop down on top of me. Experiences so terrifying I didn't want to sleep at night, but exhaustion had other ideas.

BREAKING THE CYCLE

For many years I lived without singing, without magic, and with the night terrors, until the day my kindred spirit was born to me. My little magical redhead came into this world with the same sensitivities. I could see it in her eyes. She was magic, and I was not going to take that away from her. With me, the cycle of misunderstanding, denial, and fear would be broken.

Contrary to other parents who might hush a child for singing too loudly in the grocery or who might tell them to stop singing at all, I sang to her and with her. Instead of trying to force her to not see things I knew she could, I asked her to tell me about them. Share her experiences with me.

She was just a toddler when she had her first. If you've ever seen a child have a meltdown, it was like that, just more intense and seemingly unwarranted. She would wake up in the middle of the night like she'd seen the most terrifying monster in a dream. There was no calming her. You couldn't hold her, soothe her. She had to get out of bed. She would run screaming to the couch, snuggle up on her tummy with her legs tucked underneath her like a little frog, and close her eyes. She was safe somehow on the couch. If you touched her, everything would come flooding back, so I would sit. I sat on the opposite end of the couch to let her know I was there, but I let her process her experience on her own.

If you are a parent, this may seem an unusual way to handle such a situation, but as I said, we are kindred spirits. As an empath, I could intuit what she needed. As her mother, I wanted to hold her and comfort her and bring her peace. But as someone who had the same experience, I knew she just needed her space.

CHAPTER 17 | SAY THE MAGIC WORDS

She's 13 now and talks to me about everything: her body, her fears, the things she experiences, all the irritation, annoyance, silliness that goes on in her life—her magic. And I am so grateful.

BACK TO MY REALITY

But like I said, my magic came back as I encouraged her to embrace hers. I started singing again. I started feeling again. I wandered down a path of self-exploration and discovered manifestation and ease when in a place of joy and peace.

As my mother lay in a hospice bed in 2012, getting ready to transition, I became acutely aware of exactly how powerful she was. Sitting in a chair across the room, under the dim light of a wall sconce, barely able to make out her form in the bed, I was flooded with images wholly unfamiliar to me. Images from my mother's perspective: the way she saw my father when they first met and how charmed she was by him. Cutting cake and dancing with him at their wedding reception and how pretty she felt in her little pale yellow suit dress with its white collar and cuffs. Bouncing me in her arms, tucking her cheek up against mine when I was a baby, and singing the song she had created just for me, *Mommy Calls Me Lindy*. When she held my sweet Annelise for the first time, they connected on a level no one could've perceived from the outside. It was magic, pure and unadulterated.

Huge parts of me hoped that when my mother died, I would be able to "contact" her, but I couldn't. Not for a long time, at least. Grief does that to you. Just like when tiny, ugly words kill a part of your soul, you grieve for that missing piece of you. Then one day, I wanted to talk to her so badly I imagined dialing her number at work, like I had for dozens of years. She answered my call with her typical, "Music and Theatre, this is Gayle." In the moments that followed, Mom and I carried on a conversation about everyday things. Things we would've talked about on any other day. Having that connection with her meant everything to me and reinforced my belief in everything I know to be true—magic does exist.

I share that story with people who encourage me now. In fact, I surround myself with those who believe in magic and spirit and ability.

WAIT! WHAT ABOUT MANIFESTING?

Surprisingly, or maybe not so surprising, a couple of years ago, I started asking God and the Universe for my perfect partner. All I asked for was a man who loves me for all that I am and loves my daughter like she is his own. It took a pandemic and a whole lot of faith, but he showed up last July: my human, if you will. That's another way of saying thank you, thank you, thank you for this handsome, loving, supportive, intelligent, funny hero. God gave me a second heart so I could love him the way I love Annelise.

CHAPTER 17 | SAY THE MAGIC WORDS

My hero, the one I feel like I waited my whole life for, sat with me at dinner the other night visiting with friends, listening to music, eating good food, enjoying libations. When I looked across the room at the bar and noticed a woman who, from where I was sitting, looked like she needed something. I pointed her out to him.

"What does she need, Baby?" was his immediate response.

I didn't know, really, but I was prompted to find out. I asked for his wallet and to be excused. Walking up to the bar, I got the bartender's attention and asked if the woman had already paid her tab.

"No, ma'am."

I motioned for the bartender to give it to me and paid it quickly as I leaned in slightly to get whatever she was feeling. She was disheartened, sad, lonely. And after being alone for 10 years, raising a daughter, starting a business on my own, and losing both of my parents, I knew exactly how she felt.

Sitting back down at the table, I thanked my Andrew for helping me make the connection happen.

Moments later, she wandered over and introduced herself. We'll call her Lydia.

Lydia wanted to know what made me do that, and I told her I could tell she needed something.

It didn't register.

"But how did you know?"

"I just did," I told her.

She sat down next to Andrew and asked him if I was for real. He laughed and said, "Look, as long as I've known this woman, she's felt things like this. She's the real deal if I've ever seen it."

I reached across Andrew and touched Lydia's cheek, "Inside of a year, my dear, things are going to be so much better. He was not the right one for you. You deserve so much better. For now, take care of you."

Again, "How do you know this?"

"I just do."

Turns out, 66-year-old Lydia had just broken up with the man she thought she would spend the rest of her life with. She was heartbroken and terrified that at her age, she might not find anyone else. She needed someone to show her that her magic still existed. And in the process of sharing my magic with her, my man used the magic of his tiny, beautiful words to empower me. Instead of telling me that I was stupid, he gave me everything I needed to believe in myself enough to help someone else.

I hope my tiny, lovely words helped Lydia in some small way. I hope soon she realizes she has this on her own and truly doesn't need someone to fill her life. She is completely capable of making it full on her own. But heartache and grief took that belief away from her.

CHAPTER 17 | SAY THE MAGIC WORDS

THE MORAL OF THE STORY

I believe in magic. I believe in the power of words. And I believe in you. If you and I take small steps every day to make this world a better place, the world will be a better place.

What does that mean?

Maybe it will affect sweeping change. Or maybe it will just start with us coming out from behind the veil of fear and sharing our magic with our communities at large. Maybe we can touch someone's heart with words or actions that enable them to do the same for someone else. And maybe in doing so, we'll discover the magic and the tiny, little words that live within us.

GOING FORWARD

Never, and I truly mean never, use hurtful words. Don't diminish someone's feelings by using words like stupid, ridiculous, ugly, or hush, especially with children. Don't take away their experience because you don't understand it or are fearful of it. Listen. Do research. Learn. Grow. Empower them to be free to be the magical beings they are.

Pay attention to everyone and everything around you. People deserve to know they are not alone in this life. They need reassurance without having to ask for it. They need to be filled with their own magic, whether it's the ability to see, feel, and hear things others can't; or their ability to light up a room full of people with a joke; or offering up little gifts like unexpected groceries, or dinner, or a night out away from the kids. They need to hear, "You are loved," "I see you," and "You've got this."

So, say the magic words!

Acknowledgments

Thank you, God, angels, guides, and ancestors, for Annelise and Andrew and the inspiration they provide me on a daily basis. And thank you, Melanie, for being my editor and rock.

Chapter Eighteen

Seeking Happiness in Hardship
By Katie Tryba

Katie Tryba

Katie Tryba is from Wisconsin. Her master's is in clinical mental health counseling. Her background includes special education, facilitating at day treatment for adolescents, volunteer sexual assault advocate, short stories author, and counselor.

You can reach Katie at tryba.katie+book@gmail.com.

Seeking Happiness in Hardship
By Katie Tryba

I was bleeding through my pants, feeling scared and alone, when I heard a girl run in crying and say, "My boyfriend's been shot!"

I used to believe I could only be happy if I had children. Growing up, it was ingrained in me. Sometimes our animal instincts tell us to procreate. After experiencing six years of fertility issues and two miscarriages, here is what I have learned about my partner and myself. I used to want four children, and we joked it was to add more good people to the world. It was a running joke with us after watching the movie *Idiocracy*. We know so many kind people who had terrible parents, and they chose to be good despite their upbringing. Unfortunately, the opposite also happens when growing up with physically and/or emotionally abusive parents. The cycle of abuse can repeat for generations. There is no population shortage, and there are still good people. We also wanted children to see "mini me's" of each other, but they are individuals and not necessarily going to be like us. We can have them try our interests but cannot force them to like it and need to be open to fostering their interests. There is also the guilt you feel to continue the family line by having children. Giving grandchildren or cousins to play with is not a good reason to have children. It is not your family's fault. Unfortunately, this pressure has become the norm. Luckily as our family has grown, everyone is supportive of our choices. Right now, we love

CHAPTER 18 | SEEKING HAPPINESS IN HARDSHIP

getting "kid time" through visits and spoiling our loved ones as aunt and uncle. We don't have to deal with tantrums and can just decide to leave. We still make lots of magical memories with them. My husband and I love our sleep and free time. Having children is a lifelong commitment and should not be made to please someone else. It is your responsibility to take care of them for the rest of your life, not theirs. As a couples counselor, it is a very common scenario that couples come in with problems after having children. On top of being sleep-deprived, all of your time and money go to your children. There are many issues that come up, including resentment, jealousy over the lack of attention, couple time is minimal, traveling is limited, undermining each other, putting the child before your partner, and differences in parenting styles, to name a few.

Eventually, the children grow up, leave the house, and live their own lives. You want to foster the relationship with your partner so it is strong when they leave. Using the Gottman Method, I help couples communicate better their wants, needs, wishes, and dreams. I teach them how to fight fair by avoiding the Four Horsemen: Criticism, Contempt, Defensiveness, and Stonewalling. Even if a couple gets divorced after they have children, they will see each other for the rest of their lives, and good communication will make custody easier. All parents make mistakes, but they do the best they can with what they have. No one tries to have a child because they think they will be a bad parent. Everyone is the best parent, knowing everything until they have a child.

My background is in teaching Special Education, group facilitating at a day treatment for adolescents, and counseling. I have been honored with people asking for my advice on children and teen behaviors. In high school, when I was getting ready for bed, I would always watch David Letterman's nightly top ten and then go to sleep. So I'm going to do my own Top Ten best pieces of advice for when it comes to children.

1. Children that chronically say "I don't care," especially when threatened with punishment, are really saying "I don't feel cared for by anyone." Help them feel a sense of belonging, a sense of mastery (build on their strengths), and be in service to others. Practice this phrase and use it a lot "You [describe what they did] so [how this helped others] and that was [helpful, thoughtful, or considerate etc.]. Example: You cleared the table so others could eat there. That was so helpful of you. I learned this in a Conscious Discipline training as a teacher, and it is very powerful. People have always complimented that I could work with very challenging students/clients and make it look easy. This is my secret. I took time to ask them about their interests, and I made them my helpers by giving them a sense of purpose. I praised them a lot for their help using this phrase.

2. Children and teens will minimize and maximize behaviors they do to others. It's our job to help them notice body language to pick up on those social cues. Example: She was laughing, so she didn't care that I made fun of her. When they make these excuses, ask, "Did you see her face, body, her eyes, or those tears? Those say 'I didn't like it.'" They will also blame others. They like to be in charge. Ask

CHAPTER 18 | SEEKING HAPPINESS IN HARDSHIP

them, "Is [other peer] the boss of you?" They'll say, "Well, no," and then you can add, "What could you do if you were the boss to make the situation better or treat this person with respect?" Even if they say, "I don't know," they will start to think about this and how others feel in the future.

3. Natural Consequences. When your child spills something, let them try to clean it up (even if you reclean it better when they are not watching). Teen example: when they come home late, next weekend they come home that much earlier.

4. Give Choices. Instead of getting in a power struggle argument with your child, give them two choices that you approve of to build their independence and to give them a sense of control. Child example: They do not want to pick up their toys and are throwing a tantrum. Choices: You can pick up your toys now or after supper before you watch tv. Which one do you want to do?

5. Problem Solve. When your child or teen gets in trouble, show them empathy, and ask, "What are you going to do about it?" If a teen gets a speeding ticket, say, "Oh man, that sucks. What are you going to do about it?" And depending on their answer, you can also ask, "How are you going to come up with the money for your fine?" You can start this from a young age. It is important for your child to learn the skills to problem solve on their own. Otherwise, when they are an adult, they will not know how to function without someone taking care of them or when a problem arises at a future job.

6. Emotions are good. Telling children, "Big kids don't cry," is counterproductive. Instead, say, "It's ok to be sad

(angry, any feeling word), but it's not ok to hit me or throw things at me." You can also say, "I can see you're sad (angry, any feeling word). Is there anything I can do? Like a hug, story, walk, or just some time to be alone? In conversations, try to use lots of different descriptive feeling words so as they grow up, it will be easier for them to express their feelings.

7. Positive reinforcement. This can be as simple as high fives, genuine compliments, hugs, or doing an activity they like with them (coloring, reading, playing catch). Rewards do not have to be monetary. Even when it is hard, try to find things your child is doing well to praise them on. Research shows using positive reinforcement motivates children and teens to work harder and even exceed expectations. On the other hand, using fear to persuade them, they will do the bare minimum needed to avoid the punishment. I believe in reward systems or token economies, and in my experience, they have worked very well. Some argue, "Why should children get something for work that is expected of them?" Well, great question. My reply is, "Do you work for free?" Usually, this answer is no, that you work for money. Some children are not intrinsically motivated to just do a job for no rhyme or reason. Doing reward systems or token economies is not unrealistic as it prepares children for the real world when they get a job.

8. Say what you want your children to do rather than what you don't want them to do when giving directions, instead of constant "No" or "don't." I'm not saying there's not a time or place for "No" since that is an important lesson also, not getting everything they want and learning to wait.

CHAPTER 18 | SEEKING HAPPINESS IN HARDSHIP

Example: Don't touch the stove. In fact, really young children do not understand what "don't" means and only hear the end "touch the stove." When really young, distraction might be the best bet when it comes to a dangerous situation like the stove, you can say, "Quick, come here, take the bowl and help me cook." Another example if a child hits, say, "Ouch hitting hurts. Hands are for high fives, writing, eating, playing catch, etc." (Pick one.)

9. Five minutes of undivided attention a day. Sick of your children saying that school was fine, or they don't remember what they did? This is a small thing you can do daily to build an emotional connection with them and get to know them better. Ask these questions to your children and loved ones while being fully present, making eye contact and not checking your phone during. What was something that made you feel alone today? What was something that you were proud of doing today? For fun, switch up the questions once in a while to find out more about their interests.

10. Behavior junction what's your function? (I changed the words to an old *Schoolhouse Rock* song to help me remember this). All behaviors have a function that is getting a need the child or teen wants to be met. So it is hard to just make a behavior go away; it usually needs to be replaced with a more desirable behavior that still gets that need met. Example: The child breaks a pencil or school tool every time they get mad. Replace breaking things with squeezing tightly onto a stress ball allowed at their desk. I have always been fascinated by behavior and love problem-solving them to be more desirable for all involved.

This top ten has been a lifesaver when dealing with behavior. It is the short and sweet version, so feel free to dig deeper into one or more of the techniques. I hope it helps.

Couples on the fence about having children, experiencing infertility, or suffering from miscarriages can feel isolated. My heart breaks for everyone who has had to experience painful things alone at the hospital due to Covid-19. My last miscarriage was during Covid-19. A month after my miscarriage, I continued bleeding, and I know now this is common for a lot of women, but when experiencing it for the first time, everything is terrifying and new. Our first miscarriage was very different, so the continued bleeding was concerning to me. I apologize in advance. My next details could be too much information and difficult for some to read about. I want all couples to feel empowered to share and not suffer in silence with these experiences. Skip the rest of this paragraph if you want to pass on the details. One late night I was bleeding so much it was like continuous peeing on the toilet for an hour, and meatball size clots came out of me. I cried when I felt them, not because it hurt, but terrified to think that was any part of my baby. I would go wipe, thinking it was over, and see a big clot on the toilet paper. I felt like I was retraumatizing myself with each wipe, and I would scream and cry every time. I remember it took me a long time to flush the toilet because there was so much guilt with it, and I was not sure what to do.

We called the hospital, and they said I needed to come in to be safe to check my blood levels so I do not pass out, as all women are different. We arrived very late at night and it

CHAPTER 18 | SEEKING HAPPINESS IN HARDSHIP

was freezing outside. The receptionist said my husband could not go in with me, and the waiting room was closed, so he could not stay. He did not want to leave me alone and was very worried I was bleeding to death. He offered to wait in the car, but the temperatures were -20, and she said I would be there for hours. I was terrified but didn't want anything to happen to him while waiting. I told him he should go home and I would text/call him with updates. We realized my phone was at 6% battery, and now more panic was setting in. We found a cord in the car, and the receptionist found a charger. I was so sad and felt so alone when he had to leave. He shared later that he felt terrible and cried, not knowing what was going on with me when he was at home. I followed the receptionist as she was going to bring me to a room. We saw a doctor throwing on a full-body plastic gown, and he yelled for us to get out of there. She took me back to the closed waiting room, and as I sat down, I saw my husband's car pull away. I was bleeding through my pants, feeling scared and alone, when I heard a girl run in crying and say, "My boyfriend's been shot! I think I may have been followed." I was then terrified, looking around where I could possibly hide from a shooter and wishing I was with my husband heading home where it was safe. I saw a police officer run into the ER. Next, a distraught man came in and was on the phone tearfully telling someone his son had been shot, and they wouldn't give him any information. A few more came in to sit with them, crying. I was trying to process this all. I felt guilty for being sad over my baby when this was happening to them. I realized there was enough sadness in the world for us all, and it's ok to feel our own sadness without any guilt. I texted my husband that there had been a shooting, and I was scared. My seat was getting wet from the blood. I went to the bathroom. It didn't matter that I wore a super pad; it was going through everything. I asked the receptionist if she had more pads as I was bleeding through my clothes. She said that they were getting me into a room. I followed her back and was kind of scared to look around as I didn't want to see the shooting victims. I found out the next day in the news that there were five victims. I texted my husband that I was in a room now and running tests as they can since shorthanded with all the victims. The staff was kind and apologized that I would usually be a high priority because what was happening to me was serious, but something else "crazy" was going on that had them backed up. Despite the blood loss, I didn't need a blood transfusion.

After the ultrasound, I was discharged around 5am and was supposed to follow up with my OBGYN. My husband picked me up, thankful I was ok. He called into work. There were lots of hugs, kisses, tears, and snuggles. Both too numb to cook or talk to anyone about the night, we got takeout and watched movies. I found out that the bleeding for 4-6 weeks straight with the hemorrhaging was common with miscarriage for many. Nothing about that experience felt common to me. As I shared, that didn't happen during my first miscarriage. Then I was sad, knowing I never heard details like this before and that so many must suffer in silence. I want others to know it's safe to talk about uncomfortable things and hope it can become a norm to share the scary details and have a strong support system backing you. I'm blessed to have a great group of friends in

CHAPTER 18 | SEEKING HAPPINESS IN HARDSHIP

my life. I shared the uncomfortable details with them, and you know what, they didn't react in disgust, but instead in love. In return, they all shared uncomfortable details from different parts of their lives, which made our bond stronger and everyone wiser. Everyone has their own process for healing, but if you are feeling alone, please reach out to support groups, loved ones, or counseling.

Sometimes I have a fear of missing out on the unknown, but I do not feel like that is a good enough reason to uproot our lives. I do not know what the future will bring, and our choice does not have to be set in stone. Right now, my husband and I are extremely grateful for each other. We love traveling, going to concerts, sports games, going on delicious foodie dates, board game nights, playing volleyball, and hosting lots of gatherings. I love our lifestyle and have no desire to change it for now. For other couples thinking about having children, do not be swayed by others' opinions; do what your gut tells you and allow the lifestyle you desire. Choices should not be made out of fear but out of love.

Chapter Nineteen

A Rocky Road to Parenthood
By Dorothy Welty

Dorothy Welty

Dorothy Welty is a community college administrator and teacher. She holds an MS in psychology from Illinois State University. She is passionate about the power of education to change individual lives and the world in which we live. In her free time, Dorothy enjoys meditation, hiking, kayaking, writing, baking, and a variety of other creative pursuits. You can reach Dorothy at dwelty50@gmail.com.

A Rocky Road to Parenthood and the Evolution of Parenting Wisdom that Emerged

By Dorothy Welty

Early in my childhood, I was well aware that I was different from young girls growing up in the 60s. While most girls were playing house, perusing bridal magazines, and dreaming of marriage and family, I dreamed of going to college, becoming an attorney, and eventually the first female justice on the Supreme Court. While I would not become an attorney, much less the first female Supreme Court justice, these aspirations reflected my career focus and desire for professional achievement. Marriage and family were never part of my dream.

My parents' marriage was conflict-ridden, and their parenting was harsh and authoritarian. The consistent yelling and screaming heard halfway down the block were known to the neighborhood and marked my siblings and me as undesirable playmates. As a result, outside of school, family life was isolating. We had only three extended family members on my father's side that were more of a source of additional content for arguments between my parents. Even my father's family were infrequent visitors due to the contentious environment in our home. With my parents as my only example of what marriage and parenthood entailed, I wanted none of it. I emerged from my experience growing up with so many emotional scars

CHAPTER 19 | A ROCKY ROAD TO PARENTHOOD

and baggage, becoming a parent was not part of my life plan.

Instead, I went to college and pursued a psychology major to heal myself. Though I acquired a lot of knowledge and tools through my education, looking back, it might have been more appropriate to receive serious therapy for a childhood filled with emotional trauma. Additionally, I could not make enough money to support myself with only an undergraduate education in psychology. So I remained in my more lucrative job waiting tables in Gold Coast hotels in Chicago that had paid the bills as I went to college. Upon graduation, I was overwhelmed by student loan debt, rent, insurance, and car payments. I sought distraction with romantic relationships and the nightlife in Chicago that was part of the lifestyle working in the hospitality industry.

At age 28, I moved in with a boyfriend and shortly after that found myself pregnant. Facing unwed parenthood, which still carried great shame in the 80s, I fell in line with the expectations of my conservative, Catholic upbringing and married my boyfriend. Feeling ill-prepared for parenthood, I took comfort in entering into an instant family with a man who was already a parent and seemed to be a loving and caring father to his two daughters from a previous marriage, who were ages 3 and 6 at the time. When it came to being responsible for a child, I didn't have enough confidence or resources to raise a child as a single parent. My boyfriend, now my husband, was my only support system. When I turned 18, my parents divorced. Though I had two older brothers and a younger sister, the volatility of the household we grew up in left us estranged.

I hadn't spoken to my mother since the divorce. My father threatened to disown me if I didn't marry once he knew I was pregnant, even though he didn't approve of my boyfriend or our cohabitation.

Five months after the wedding, I became a parent. It had been a difficult childbirth, and I remember today like it was yesterday how overwhelmed and utterly unprepared I felt to be responsible for another human life. We brought the baby home to a cockroach-infested apartment in a Hispanic neighborhood on the edge of a gang-ridden area of the city. I had no family to help with the baby. My husband took our only car and was off to school and work 15 hours a day. My great sense of duty and responsibility carried me through the long days of caring for my son. I shed many tears between the diaper changes and feedings, mourning the life of professional accomplishment that had always been my dream.

Despite being one of the last people I felt should be charged with the responsibility of caring for another human life, I was blessed with an adorable son that drew in the attention of any individual that even glanced his way. He was absolutely a magnetic personality. It took around 6 or 8 months, but one day when I had him on the floor on a blanket changing his diaper, he won me over. I remember marveling at what a complete and unique little person he was. It was so clear to me at that moment that he was a unique spirit alive with life, and I needed to do right by him to the best of my ability. I still didn't know what I was doing, but I figured if I could do a few things differently than my parents had done, it would be a vast improvement over the parenting I had received.

CHAPTER 19 | A ROCKY ROAD TO PARENTHOOD

I took inventory of the good I could take from my childhood. There were three things I valued that had been instilled in me by my parents despite their flaws. My parents had raised me with integrity, a sense of personal responsibility, and a strong work ethic. I would pass these on.

I also took inventory from my childhood on what not to do as a parent. Instead of expecting my son to enter into my experience, I was determined to enter into his experience to the best of my ability. I would look to who he was as a unique spirit. Even from infancy, I could see he knew how to draw people in to engage with him. I observed he was always on the move, from how early he tumbled around in the womb to how daring he was in his play activities. I looked for signs of his interests and did everything I could to support them.

My son was a sheer joy to parent. He was a compliant, cheerful, and engaging child. Everybody liked him, parents, peers, girls, teachers, and coaches. By the time he was nine years old, I had earned a degree in education and a graduate degree in psychology. I had become a college instructor. My husband and I had a lovely home in a great community with good schools. We had a large circle of friends, many of whom viewed us as the ideal family. In many ways, my life was what so many young girls of my generation from the sixties had visualized.

While so much of my parenting approach revolved around nurturing my son's unique spirit, I took a great deal of credit for raising such a wonderful son. Despite having had my son as a result of an unplanned, unwanted pregnancy under difficult economic circumstances, this glorious outcome had me thinking about having another child. I wondered what it would be like to have a child under the more ideal circumstances. I had enjoyed parenting more than I ever thought I would. Ten years after having my first son, I gave birth to a second son.

To say my second son was different from the first is an understatement. My second child was more introverted and extremely disagreeable from a very young age. His first word was "no," and he was very adept at using it. He was the epitome of the strong-willed child, and he made it clear that he would march to the beat of his own drum.

Twenty-two years after choosing marriage over raising a child as a single parent, I would end my marriage and raise my second son, who had just turned 12 as a single parent. Little did I know that my second child was to be my greatest teacher yet. My second son would challenge all I thought I knew about parenting. He would reject integrity, a strong work ethic, and personal responsibility. He would break my rules as well as the school's rules. He would be disagreeable and non-compliant at every turn. He would reject expectations and all attempts at discipline.

Had I ever been a good parent, or had my first-born son simply complied with expectations and discipline? Was this the job of a parent to discipline a child into compliance with one's expectations?

As I turned 60 this year, I received the news that I would graduate to the role of a grandparent as my granddaughter arrived into the world. I do not doubt that my understanding of parenting will evolve as I observe my son and

CHAPTER 19 | A ROCKY ROAD TO PARENTHOOD

daughter-in-law embark on their child-rearing journey. The following principles are a few pieces of enduring wisdom through my parenting journey. I hope to embody this wisdom by example as I embrace my role as a grandmother and continue to be forever mother to my sons.

Foster emotional intelligence

Schools will teach children reading, writing, and arithmetic, and some will also touch upon skills involved in emotional intelligence. Still, it is parents who are the primary educators for emotional intelligence. In his book, *Emotional Intelligence*, Daniel Goleman identified five components of emotional intelligence that can be taught to children and can continue to develop throughout life: Self-awareness, self-regulation, internal motivation, empathy, and social skills. Self-awareness involves teaching a child to recognize and understand their emotions and their effects on others. Self-regulation consists of helping children learn to control or redirect emotions. Internal motivation is the propensity to pursue goals and persevere in those efforts. Empathy, or the ability to understand others' feelings, is also a necessary life skill. Finally, children need social skills to identify common ground, manage relationships and build social networks. Growing up in a home filled with conflict, emotional regulation, and social skill development was not fostered, and I suffered tremendously.

Practice and teach kindness, gratitude, humility, integrity, and forgiveness

Virtuous behavior builds character and has the power to change the world. While there are many virtues worth practicing and teaching to children, I have found these five to be particularly powerful in my life. The only virtue of the five that was an example to me from my parents was the virtue of integrity. Learning through their powerful example of integrity has served me well in my life. I acquired the other four virtues through the hardship I endured because of their absence in my life. These are virtues I hope I have passed on to my sons and exemplify as a grandparent.

Provide an environment that fosters self-discipline

While I won't go as far as to say we should never discipline children, I have learned it is far more valuable once a child hits the age of reason to focus on providing an environment that will help children learn the value of self-discipline. Too much parental discipline creates compliance driven by external motivation. Teaching and supporting self-discipline in a child becomes an internally motivated practice that can also become a habit. Self-discipline also builds character and fosters self-esteem.

Build connection

I think children crave connection. If parents can connect with their children, it lessens the need for control. As a mother of two sons, building connections was not always easy. In the teen years, I found being present, looking for opportunities to enter into their experience, and making

CHAPTER 19 | A ROCKY ROAD TO PARENTHOOD

quality time centered around food was helpful. While I didn't always succeed, I knew the strong connection I had fostered in the early years with my younger son would be a foundation we could return to once we survived and recovered from some of the challenging teen years when connection was missing.

Help discover what stirs their soul

My reflection on my parenting of my sons supporting their interests was something I feel I did well. Their feedback to me as adults has been confirming. When I was growing up, children played outside. There were more informal games in the neighborhood versus the organized activities available today. However, most children were involved in one or two lessons, sports, or activities. I had not had those opportunities. I spent many years of my childhood begging for piano lessons to no avail. So, when I became a parent, I committed to providing my sons opportunities to pursue their interests. I told them to explore their interests, find what stirs their soul, and then find a way to get paid for it, and their livelihood would never feel like work.

Recognize a child's uniqueness

In the field of human development, there is a concept called goodness-of-fit. It is a concept that applies to adapting one's parenting to a child's temperament to foster the best adaptive outcomes for the child in their development. In parenting my two sons, I quickly discovered what had worked for one would not necessarily work for the other.

Every child is a unique soul, here for a special purpose. By acknowledging their uniqueness, parents can create the best conditions for children to rise to their potential.

Give your child an excellent example of a loving partnership

Having two loving parents who love, respect, and support one another through all the joys and challenges of life is such an advantage in a child's development. Without receiving that precious gift in my upbringing and failing to provide the example of a loving partnership to my sons, I decided my children would rather come from a broken home than live in one. I know that I lived in a broken home for my entire childhood, during which time my siblings and I often wished our parents would divorce. Though I also failed to provide my sons an excellent example of a loving partnership between their parents, I did choose to use strength and courage to go it alone, forgive my spouse and demonstrate the capacity for resilience to my sons.

Love unconditionally

I grew up with what Carl Rogers coined conditions of worth, conditions I felt I must meet to receive love from my parents. Conditions of worth bred anxiety and insecurity in me that took decades to overcome. A child is worthy of love and acceptance simply because they exist. Unconditional love also fosters healthy development. While both of my sons, at different times, put my unconditional love to the test, a stronger bond resulted from my ability to deliver

CHAPTER 19 | A ROCKY ROAD TO PARENTHOOD

unconditional love when even my sons didn't feel worthy due to their own choices. I knew I didn't always have to agree or condone my children's choices as a parent, but I needed to make sure they know that I will always be their greatest cheerleader. Even at their lowest point, I will be there to pick them up, help dust them off and cheer them on.

In the words of Maya Angelou, "I've learned that people will forget what you said, people will forget what you did, but people will never forget how you made them feel." This statement holds for our children as well. If your eyes light up when your child walks in the room, it tells your child you are present, you acknowledge them, and you delight in their very existence. That is a feeling they will never forget.

CHAPTER 19: A ROCKY ROAD TO PARENTHOOD

Chapter Twenty

Soul Signs
By Kristen West

Kristen West

I am an Autumn-loving Midwesterner who is gratefully surrounded by loving family and friends, a supportive husband, and two beautiful children. When not at work, I can generally be found with my nose in a book and two very needy cats in my lap.

I am a practicing veterinarian and adore my job, but I have always yearned to write. I decided that it is never too late to follow my dream, and I am thrilled to be contributing to this book. kwestdvm@aol.com

Soul Signs
By Kristen West

On my way to church on Easter morning 2011, I sped past a lone bald eagle perched on a bare tree branch. In this blink of an eye, my heart lifted, and my life changed.

A month before Easter, my father had passed away suddenly. His death was devastating, unexpected, and difficult to fathom. Memories of this time in my life are blurred and saturated with emotion and turmoil. The one thing that stands out is my subsequent daily prayer to God to show me a bald eagle if my dad was okay and safe with Him.

I don't know why I picked the eagle as the sign I was seeking. It wasn't an animal that held special significance for me at the time, nor for my dad, as far as I knew. Though this has changed in subsequent years, eagles were not commonly seen in our area in 2011. My dad and I did share a love of animals, so I knew it had to be an animal that I needed to see. The eagle just came to mind. Since eagles were rarely spotted, a sighting would be significant to me. Eagles also had always seemed so majestic and free, and I imagined them as existing in a realm closer to God.

I was also not a big believer in signs at the time, at least not in those sent for me. I wholly believed that God had reached out through signs to multiple people in the Bible, and I believed that "other people" received heavenly signs or angel interventions daily. I just hadn't specifically ever requested one, and though I felt God in my life in other ways previously, this was my first request for a specific sign.

CHAPTER 20 | SOUL SIGNS

Compounding my skepticism that God would want to answer my request was the reality that I had not been a perfect Catholic in the preceding years. Family pain and sadness over life's twists and turns had led me away from the church and daily prayer. I had allowed myself to falter in my faith, so I felt exceptionally undeserving of spiritual intervention in my life. Nevertheless, I held enough hope that I had searched the sky daily in the days and weeks following Dad's death.

That Easter morning, as I sailed past the bird in question, I got enough of a glimpse to make me think that maybe I had seen an eagle. Maybe God had answered my prayer! I wasn't immediately sure, as the bird I saw looked like an eagle but did not have a white head. I knew that juvenile bald eagles did not develop white feathers on their heads for a few years, but wouldn't it have been a more obvious answer to a prayer to show me a "typical" bald eagle? As I was busy questioning the Lord's signs for me, I did acknowledge that the moment I glimpsed the bird, my heart filled with peace, and the heavy weight that had lain on my chest had lifted. My spirit soared before I tried to pull it back down with my doubts.

For some unfathomable reason, God had patience and kindness for me. Two weeks later, while on a routine trip into a local town, I saw not one but two bald eagles on a tree branch near the road. One had the white head that I was longing to see, and its companion was a juvenile bald eagle like I had seen on Easter morning. I pulled off the road, and between tears of joy and awe, I stared at the birds for about ten minutes until they flew away. My prayer had been answered threefold. The Lord was listening to me, communicating with me, and my dad was, without a doubt, okay. I was comforted and amazed and deeply humbled.

This experience changed me. I felt a closeness to the Divine that was inexplicable. I felt so humbled that God would answer my prayer in such a profound way. God was so real to me, and I knew that He was watching over Dad and us. I shouldn't have needed to see something physical to know that God was there, but it was faith-affirming.

The bald eagle has become a symbol for me, not only of my dad but of God's great love for us. Every time I see an eagle, I give thanks, and I think of my dad. Coincidence or not, eagles had often appeared when I needed my dad or thought of him over the years. I believe they have become a way for me to feel his love.

Although eagles have become a special sign for me of the Lord, I also see Him in nature and other creatures, especially other birds. There have been countless times that I have asked for God to hear me, and I saw a bird or other animal. Red-tailed hawks and great blue herons have often appeared as an answer to prayer, but I see God in all creatures.

Another specific time in my life that God has sent me signs had to do with my sister. My sister had estranged herself from the family seventeen years ago. Her reasons were never fully explained, and her absence affected us deeply in many ways. I had tried initially to contact her, but after multiple rejections, I had let it be. The situation has been devastating, as she is my only sibling and her children my only blood niece and nephew. The break in the family was especially heartbreaking to my parents, and I was left to try to hold us together. I spent years with many feelings on the subject, including pain, disappointment, grief, anger, loss, pride, and disquieted acceptance.

Since the movie *Frozen* came out in 2013, the sister storyline and musical score hit a chord with me, and I can't watch the film without crying. I wondered if my sister saw the movie and felt the same way. Pride and fear of rejection kept me from reaching out to her for many years. Anger also at her absence during the death of our father kept me idle.

CHAPTER 20 | SOUL SIGNS

For whatever reason, this movie kept coming into my mind. I had a strong feeling that it could help bridge the gap between us. It took seven years and increasingly nagging thoughts about this movie to make me consider reaching out. I decided to pray about it, and I boldly asked for three signs to show me if I was supposed to reach out to my sister. I don't remember if I specifically asked for *Frozen*-themed signs, but that is what I got! The same day that I requested these signs, I got them, and then some. I saw an Elsa statue in the middle of a sports memorabilia store with no other Disney items in sight. I heard a *Frozen* song playing in a random book store. I saw *Frozen* posters and collectible items in every store we entered that day. As happened with previous spirit signs, my heart knew that these were for me as much as my mind did. It's hard to explain, but I felt each one in my gut in a physical way. I did not need to question it.

Since I was not yet ready to put aside my pride and open this emotional Pandora's box with my sister, I still didn't reach out. I prayed again on my way to work the week later for one more sign. A double rainbow was in the sky, and it was not raining, nor sunny out. The rainbow appeared in front of me and "led" me to the exit ramp. I felt it and decided that it was up to me to act on these signs.

I reached out to my sister by sending her the movie *Frozen* with a simple note, "Do you want to build a snowman?" I sent it knowing that it may lead to another closed door, but it opened up a communication line between us. Things may never be how I would like them to be, but we are communicating, and it is a beginning. I also know that God must have wanted this to happen as He led me along this path.

Although I know that these signs mentioned above were incredible and direct answers to prayer, there are so many times that I have asked for signs and not gotten them or did not get the answers that I wanted. I know now, however, without a doubt, that God is listening. I will not get everything I want, but I believe that when I ask Him with a humble heart and good intention, He listens. I have become more open to ways that He may be communicating with me. I have seen and heard Him through other people, animals, nature, songs, images, and so much more. Once I experienced Him in this way, my eyes were open and eager to see more. I look now for signs everywhere and often find God when I would least expect to.

Recently, I have been considering trying my hand at writing. I have always wanted to be a writer, but I decided to pursue a career in science instead and work very happily as a veterinarian. I have always felt an affinity for animals, so I do believe that this is the course I should have taken, but I have never stopped yearning to write. I discussed this recently with my mother, who happens to be an excellent writer and former English teacher. As we were talking, we saw eight to ten bluebirds flying around our car. They were perched above the car, in bushes and trees next to the car, and flew overhead. I have learned enough from previous doubts to know a sign when I see one. It was beautiful and remarkable, and I decided to pursue writing actively. I have started to submit short stories to online writing contests. My mother and I are also working together on an idea for a novel. We both left that experience believing that we had a sign in the form of bluebirds.

I also believe that a sign led me to submit this story for inclusion in this book. When I saw that *Enduring Wisdom* was the title, I immediately assumed that I had nothing to offer on this topic and navigated away from the email. When I rejected it, my stomach immediately became very upset. I decided to listen to my body and went back to sign up. I know that I need to travel where God leads. As faith grows, it is increasingly easier to listen to the

CHAPTER 20 | SOUL SIGNS

signs. Maybe these reflections on God's signs will affect someone else who also lives with doubt.

If I can impart any wisdom, it would be that we are not alone. A higher power is with us and around us and close enough to hear us and respond. Life has its ups and downs, and faith waxes and wanes. God is there through it all, and we can call upon Him. The times that He has answered my prayers have put the times He didn't seem to answer prayer into a different perspective. I can go forward knowing that God walks with me and with all of us. We can seek Him in all things, as He created all things. His signs abound if we are willing to open our eyes, hearts, and minds to His wondrous ways.

www.ingramcontent.com/pod-product-compliance
Lightning Source LLC
Chambersburg PA
CBHW071307110426
42743CB00042B/1199